Crying For Freedom Is Not Being Free.

*…Make your life a meaningful one by standing up and fight for what you believe in and be unrestricted in doing so.*

# Table of Contents

# Author's Note

In his speech in 1967 by Malcolm X in the last year of his life, he stated that, "we declare our right on this earth to be a man, to be a human being, to be respected as a human being, to be given the rights of a human being in this society, on this earth, in this day, which we intend to bring into existence by any means necessary.[1]" So, utilizing Malcolm X quotes, I believe that we must attain freedom in our lifetime on this earth by any means necessary. You can't let anyone stand in your way in your quest for freedom. Jamaican Reggae singer Beres Hammond's song "No Apology" let us know that, "we only got one life to live and we should make no apology.[2]" Live your life the way you want (not infringing on others) with no apology to no one, because your life cycle comes around only once, and we know that the freedom we want must attain by any means necessary.

The first amendment of our constitution is the law referring to our freedom. It stated that, "Congress shall make no law respecting an establishment of religion or prohibiting the free exercise thereof; or abridging the freedom of speech, or of the press; or the right of the people peaceably to assemble, and to petition the government for a redress of grievances.[3]"

---

[1] *BlackPast, B. (2007, October 15) (1964) Malcolm X's Speech at the Founding Rally of the Organization of Afro-American Unity. Retrieved from https://www.blackpast.org/african-american-history/1964-malcolm-x-s-speech-founding-rally-organization-afro-american-unity/*

[2] *Hammond, B. (June 18, 2010). No Apology [Beres Hammond]. Reggae Gold 2010 [Album]. Queens, New York: VP Records. (June 18, 2010)*

[3] *First Amendment of the United States Constitution. Constitution.congress.gov https://constitution.congress.gov/constitution/amendment-1/*

Our constitution guarantees us the following freedoms: religion, expression, assembly, and the right to petition.  It prevents our Congress from promoting one religion over another and restricting individual religious practice.  Freedom of expression guarantees that an individual can speak freely, and it prohibits Congress from limiting us from speaking freely.  It also guarantees the rights of every citizen to assemble peaceably and to petition their government.

Claude Brown, the author of *Manchild in the Promised Land*, one of my favorite books, stated that, "I didn't have any dreams of becoming anything. All I knew for certain was that I had my fears. I suppose just about everybody else knew the same thing.  They had their dreams, though, and I guess that's what they had over me. As time went by, I was sorry for the people whose dreams were never realized.[4]"  Whenever you pass by a place of burial, just imagine all those that died without realizing their dream and was never free. Having our freedom doesn't mean you are free.  You have to be careful about how you exercise the use of this word.  You have to understand that having freedom is a choice to do what is right and not do whatever you want to infringe on others' rights.

Whenever the word or the subject freedom ascends in your thoughts, you must define what it means to you.  It has to be your definition of what is right without infringing on the rights of others. Because until you determine what freedom means to

---

[4] Brown, Claude. *Manchild in the Promised Land*

# Acknowledgments

This world is truly a wonderful place when everyone is willing to be involved and make the weight one carries become lighter and manageable.

I will always give thanks to the God of my life for the great things he continues to do in my life. I am still a work in progress. Thank you, God, for the great things you have done in my life, and I will continue to follow your direction. When I look at the past and the present, I know the best is yet to come. You have made the weight I carry much lighter and manageable.

For instance, I want to thank my fore-parents, my maternal grandparents, for their sacrifice in providing me that educational roof over my head and their religious and paternal guidance. They took over where my mother started and proceeded without hindrance. They each dedicate their time teaching me the things that will guide me even to this day.

To my mother, "the miracle lady," the pillar of my strength was and still plays a significant role in my life. My heart is in heaven.

To those individuals, too many names to mention, I would like to acknowledge their efforts in educating me on how to proceed in life. They have dedicated their time teaching me about my existence in this world. Thanks to the generosity of those who went out of their ways to make this book a success.

I will not become a prisoner of my past. It is just a lesson that I have learned, and it is not a life sentence handed down to me. I was born free, and I will die free. Over these years, I have learned to understand that the chains will break that bind us as soon as we rise, and no one will hold us down anymore.

Much gratitude of thanks to all, especially generated from my heart honestly and sincerely. Remember, in life; freedom is not externally; it is the way you feel inside about yourself. Therefore, crying for freedom is not being free.

you, you are not going to exercise the use of this word appropriately. It will only be an illusion of your imagination.

# Introduction

L iving your life, the way you want, is being free because freedom may mean many things to each individual. You must live life by pursuing your passion and working in the profession you love. For most of us, freedom is doing what you love, and it should be one of our highest priorities. If you are an individual who loves to read, the outcome from this, is not just about ways to change you; it is all about helping you find ways to change your attitudes toward what you want out of life. I believe that every person should start studying and reading about the inner perception of themself. It is not encouraging to sit back and wait for others to fight for you because of the struggle you have always begun internally with every individual and exported externally to others in your community.

As a race, Africans face an identity crisis and sometimes don't accept who they are. If we don't know who we are, how will we find ourselves understanding who we are and becoming? You see, as African, we were violently removed from our motherland and taken all over the world, and now we are only identifying ourselves to where we abode and not straight up African. For example, we call ourselves Black Americans because we are black and living in that country. If we see our future as Africans, then we have got to help that nation's potential and let the world see that being African is not negative. Therefore, being an African, you are free because it is your nature to live and continue to fight that external source that is denying our freedom. An example of myself; the more I read, understand, and observe what it is to be a man of African Heritage in a world controlled by others and not fighting for my freedom the more I am free from heartache. You should not sit back and wait for freedom to come your way and not fighting for it. Frederick Douglass stated in his speech delivered at the *West India Emancipation* at Canandaigua, New York, on August 3, 1857. This speech was dated back when freedom for African Americans was just a state of mind because they were slaves. Here we have a man who is stating what he feels inside, externally without fear. He stated that, "The general sentiment of mankind is that a man who will not fight for himself, when he has the means of doing so, is not worth being fought for by others, and this sentiment is just. [5]" You can't just sit by and watch others fight your fight while you lay up in your home sputtering words of freedom with inaction. He further stated in his speech, "For a man who does not value freedom for himself will never value it for others or put himself to any inconvenience to gain it for others. Such a man, the world says, may lie down until he has sense enough to stand up. It is useless and cruel to put a man on his legs, if the next moment his head is to be brought against a curbstone.[6]"

You have got to stop being governed by your internal hopes or your fears. Yes, you can have hopes


[5] *BlackPast, B. (2007, January 25) (1857) Frederick Douglass, "If There Is No Struggle, There Is No Progress". Retrieved from https://www.blackpast.org/african-american-history/1857-frederick-douglass-if-there-no-struggle-there-no-progress/*

[6] *BlackPast, B. (2007, January 25) (1857) Frederick Douglass, "If There Is No Struggle, There Is No Progress". Retrieved from https://www.blackpast.org/african-american-history/1857-frederick-douglass-if-there-no-struggle-there-no-progress/*

and fears, but living by them will control your life, and your struggle for freedom will be discouraged.  Let's face it, sometimes fighting for what you want will lead to living dangerously or near the edge of the precipice of non-activity.  At least your life will not be depicted as a person who lacks wants but never tried to achieve an exciting and glamorous endeavor.  If you fight, it might inspire others to follow, and more fighters will build an army that will help each other through good and bad times.  If you lose, at least you know that you have to find another way through that obstacle that is in your way.  Sooner or later, you will find a way through, over, or around those humans made obstacles.  You should not sit idly on your ass hugging those chains of fears that bind your freedom, nor should you allow others to fight for your freedom without helping yourself.   Malcolm X stated that, "you can't separate peace from freedom because no one can be at peace unless he has his freedom.[7]"

It is not for you to be governed by your hopes or our fears while searching for that not so elusive right to think, act and speak, which is always within your reach, but yet you make it so far because you fail to reach out and grab it. However, you can cry every day in our suffering without surveying your position during your struggle.  This struggle is going on in your mind between being a slave internally or fighting for your freedom externally. If you have not encouraged yourself to develop your inner feeling of wanting to be

---

[7] Malcolm X Quotes. (n.d.). BrainyQuote.com. Retrieved January 4, 2021, from BrainyQuote.com Web site: https://www.brainyquote.com/quotes/malcolm_x_387554

free, you will continue to live in the past.  You have to feed yourself positively that will help you not to look back to those past actions that are gone, and you can't change.  You have to transform yourself into the present that will impact your future positively.

The right that you have to act, speak, or think without hindrance or restraint is your choice of freedom, and you should let no one infringe on them. You can't have that ostrich mentality, by burying your head in the sand and pretend nothing is happening around you.  If you do, the world will pass you by.

# Defining Your Freedom

**M**alcolm X stated that "Nobody can give you freedom. Nobody can give you equality or justice or anything. If you're a man, you take it.[8]" Without violence, you will have to let others know that you want your freedom.  What is freedom? While doing my research for this book, I came across a June 27, 2012 article in Live Science written by Katherine Gammon, a freelance science writer, *"What Is Freedom."*  I am using this definition from Live Science to infuse my argument to help better open the flood gate of my deliverance of this word, not the action.  The definition by Gammon stated that, "Freedom is the power or right to act, speak, or think as one wants without hindrance or restraint, and the absence of a despotic government.[9]"

When it comes to freedom, you have to ask yourself about this definition.  Can you say that this definition is a factual one when you compare it to your daily lives, or is it just meaning for those in control of your daily lives?  You must not forget that the First Amendment of the United States Constitution guarantees your freedom.  The First Amendment of our Constitutions stated that, "Congress shall make no law respecting an establishment of religion or prohibiting the free exercise thereof; or abridging the freedom of speech, or of the press; or the right of the

---

[8] *Malcolm X Quotes. (n.d.). BrainyQuote.com. Retrieved January 17, 2021, from BrainyQuote.com Web site: https://www.brainyquote.com/quotes/malcolm_x_387554*

[9] *Gammon, K. (June 27, 2012). What Is Freedom. Livescience.com. https://www.livescience.com/21212-what-is-freedom.html*

people peaceably to assemble, and to petition the Government for a redress of grievances.[10]"

You have to make the path to achieving our freedom easy.  It should not be a secret that you have to spend your precious time worrying about how others feel about it.  It is ok to have that nervous feeling when you are alone in your thoughts.  If you want to be a success, you have to believe that successful people should never let fears overcome them when they are fighting for freedom.  To be successful in your drive, you must look fear dead in the eyes, go over it, or run it over.  You should face your fear and rise to the challenge of your dream of freedom.

When facing your fear, you must have a clear objective on how to defeat it without violence.  You must be clear on what you want, and the direction or path you want to take to get there.  Whatever it takes without violence, to get to your destination, you must have your own clear intentions not the ideas of others. In his *"I have a dream"* speech, the Rev. Dr. Martin Luther King Jr. stated that, "… there is something that I must say to my people, who stand on the warm threshold which leads into the palace of justice: in the process of gaining our rightful place, we must not be guilty of wrongful deeds. Let us not seek to satisfy our thirst for freedom by drinking from the cup of bitterness and hatred.[11]"  In the process of moving

---

[10] *First Amendment of the United States Constitution*

[11] *King, Martin Luther, Jr.(August 28, 1963). "I Have a Dream," Address Delivered at the March on Washington for Jobs and Freedom*

towards your destination in searching for or fighting for freedom, you must use the power of love to resist negativity for your freedom.

When others attack your vision, you must remain strong because it is your dream or that mental picture in your mind. This will be your Vision of why you want that freedom, and it should be personal to you. Your mission in trying to obtain your freedom should not be that impossible dream. You should not let the hate of others drive out your dream because this is your long-term plan to accomplish what is important to you in life-your dream for freedom. Those who resist, or even attack your vision won't succeed because of your will, strong determination and your drive. You are responsible for your freedom and nobody else.

So, accept responsibility and back your dream by utilizing all the tools in your toolbox with considerable action, not reaction or nonaction. You must follow that vivid painted picture of your magnificent dream you so adequately created. This will allow you not to give up on your dream for freedom when you face apparently insurmountable obstacles. Follow the ideas of Martin Luther King Jr. He stated that, "In the process of gaining our rightful place we must not be guilty of wrongful deeds. Let us not seek to satisfy our thirst for freedom by drinking from the cup of bitterness and hatred. We must forever conduct our struggle on the high plane of dignity and discipline. We must not allow our creative protest to degenerate into physical violence. Again, and again we must rise to the majestic heights of meeting physical force with soul force.[12]"

---

[12] King, Martin Luther, Jr.(August 28, 1963). "I Have a Dream," Address Delivered at the March on Washington for Jobs and Freedom

# Your Moral Compass

When you look at the personal values that guide you in making your decisions, it is your integrity and personal responsibility they are your moral compass in life. Your moral compass always points to the true North (the freedom you seek). It will help to take you on the direct path towards your desire designation. Your moral compass will also help guide you on that path you decide to bring to your selected goal: freedom. Your moral compass is the metaphor that describes your approach to choosing freedom of right and not wrong that offers a framework to your guide to the actions you take. Your moral compass encompassed your values and belief system, the principles you set, and your goal to obtain your freedom. These components are the central part that motor your engine through that path to your objective as the guiding system.

Your moral compass embodied the values and belief system that are important for your journey in life. It is your system of beliefs that allow you to decided what is right and wrong. The value that you share helps you to determine good from bad in your decision-making process. As you immerse and detect if changes have to be made, you need to modify your values. What may have been right yesterday may need to be modified today to suit your journey for tomorrow. To determine whether your current values are up to par for your journey, you must place them in order of significance. It would be best if you let your values define your freedom before you can see it. The following statement from *Mentalhelp.net* article, *Values and Morals Clarification: Value Changes,* stated that, "Moral understanding is not the only thing that changes as people mature. People's values tend to change over time as well. Values that suited you as a child change as you become a young adult, form relationships and make your way in the world.[13]" So, to achieve the destiny that you desire, you need to allow your values to progress to guide your moral compass down the right path to your freedom. You must learn to change your values, if necessary, to achieve your freedom.

Your sets of beliefs about what is right and wrong and true and false represent the base of your life and help with the direction and path you take. You will have to learn to use your belief systems to help you to cope with what you encounter in your life. Yes, as a rational being, your belief systems will be your guide, and your survival to the goal you set in obtaining your freedom should be based on ensuring your coping mechanism. This will play a significant role in molding your mind over time. According to *Tim Rettig's* article, *Belief Systems: what they are and how they affect you,* in Medium.com, stated that, "Your belief system is the invisible force behind your behavior. Together with other factors such as your personality, your genetic set up and your habits, your belief system is one of the strongest forces that affects

---

[13] *Values and Morals Clarification: Value Changes. (n.d.)*
*https://www.mentalhelp.net/self-help/values-and-morals-changes/*

any decision that you are making.[14]" It would be best if you multiplied the invisible force behind your behavior in seeking freedom. It will push your moral compass in the right direction.

The former first lady of the United States, Michelle Obama, stated that, "I have learned that as long as I hold fast to my beliefs and values - and follow my own moral compass - then the only expectations I need to live up to are my own.[15]" You have to understand that your moral compass only can direct you in the right direction; the decision to follow that direction is really up to you. The sources of information that you gather on your way to the goal that you set will help you to apply it to the situation that will solidify the direction of your moral compass. You must be sincere with your inner self to know and understand what you can do and not repeat previous mistakes. Albert Einstein, the famous physicist, stated that, "The only source of knowledge is experience[16]" Therefore, the facts and skills you acquired through your experience and education will help to keep you on the defined part of your journey.

When you make your judgment in helping your moral compass, it must be based on your rational thought. You cannot travel on a path where irrational

---

[14] Rettig, T. (December 17, 2017). Belief Systems: what they are and how they affect you. medium.com https://medium.com/intercultural-mindset/belief-systems-what-they-are-and-how-they-affect-you-1cd87aa775ff

[15] Michelle Obama Quotes. (n.d.). BrainyQuote.com. Retrieved February 5, 2021, from BrainyQuote.com Web site:
https://www.brainyquote.com/quotes/michelle_obama_791345

[16] Albert Einstein Quotes. (n.d.). BrainyQuote.com. Retrieved February 5, 2021, from BrainyQuote.com Web site:
https://www.brainyquote.com/quotes/albert_einstein_148778

feelings such as anger shift that needle from the known direction. You must harness and disregard all irrational feelings and approaches that hold you back from making better moral decisions. Learn to be healthy by letting go of what does not work and be patient to wait for what works. Your moral compass must be your guide on the journey toward that goal-your freedom, no deviation. Your inner thoughts can be the shield of protection when there are boundaries of positivity. This will give you the confidence to move ahead without worrying about your surroundings. That moral compass is your guide.

Building a strong positive foundation early in life gives you the right guidance when pessimism comes along the way. Your sense of self-worth will not be dependent on the outside world but only on your internal feeling. Feeling built from an earlier foundation will help guide the functioning moral compass that is more grounded and focused on a more productive life. Having a more nurturing and positive relationship with the environment and people around you will positively maximize your contributions. In other words, you are giving back more to gain that freedom you so desire. Giving more will help determine that moral compass will always be your guide.

So, to gain that freedom you so desire, it helps create that community where common values and aspirations are shared with others. The bond that you created in your community will allow the members as those external forces to guide your moral compass in your search for freedom. Your engagement with others in your active search for all those values that will guide your journey following your moral compass helps to construct healthier societies for us to live. The community where you live is there to help, not leading you in searching for your values and belief system that are important in your journey in life.

# Blaming Others for Your Shortcomings

David Goggins, a Navy SEAL plus other specialized training, an ultramarathon runner, triathlete, motivational speaker, and also author. In his book *"Can't Hurt Me,"* which I read twice, was my inspiration to become a writer. Not to say that staying in shape was not another goal of mine. I do believe that staying in shape to demanding my freedom, is the key to self-development. His quote, "I turned off the television and thought about my own life. It was a life devoid of any drive and passion, but I knew if I continued to surrender to my fear and my feelings of inadequacy, I would be allowing them to dictate my future forever.[17]"

The burdens of wanting to be free while living in a free country does not guarantee a life that is free at all. While trying to attain that sometimes elusive state of mind-freedom can generate a constant struggle. The more struggle you have, the stronger the fight should be in trying to achieve your goal. Let us not forget that those hindrances to your freedom do not only come from your government but some from other people, maybe your next-door neighbors. You have to understand that the freedom that you seek is precious. Not because it liberates you from those lifelong restraints that situation has placed on you, but to free your mind, body, and soul that will help in your

---

[17] *Excerpt From: David Goggins. "Can't Hurt Me." Apple Books.*
*https://books.apple.com/us/book/cant-hurt-me/id1446028392*

effort toward life's central purpose-the freedom you seek. You must not surrender to your fear and your feelings of inadequacy because you have to make life in your image of freedom. Once you start succumbing to your fear, it will increase and begin gaining a foothold in your lives. This fear will then magnify, and its presence will become uncontrollable. Therefore, your uncontrollable fear will control your present state, affecting you mentally, emotionally, and physically. It will then eliminate the keys to help remove those chains and strengthen the hold to bind your freedom.

Victor E. Frankl in his book *"Man's Search for Meaning"* stated that, "Even when people in difficult circumstances appear to have no options available, they retain the freedom to choose how they will respond to their suffering.[18]" Freedom is an important choice that represents your rights-the individual, to make your own decision without being subjective to the authority of others. You can't steal second base without being on first base; and you can't get to first base without getting a hit. So, your choice of freedom allow you to be able select your own course of action and your personal preferences. This course should not violate or infringe on others right. Your freedom of choice should not trump the choice of another. But you shouldn't let others bully you from achieving your freedom. Remember you can't blame others for your shortcoming.

---

[18] *Excerpt From: Instaread. "Man's Search for Meaning: by Viktor E. Frankl Key Takeaways, Analysis & Review." Apple Books. https://books.apple.com/us/book/mans-search-for-meaning-by-viktor-e-frankl-key-takeaways/id1042804725*

Your freedom is not around the bend, nor is it down the road. It is right in front of you. As a matter of fact, your freedom is internal. So, let it out and follow it. Your external freedom is the goal that you set, and you will not let nothing stand in your way in obtaining it. If you suppress your freedom internally it will die with you. Make haste while the sun is shining and get over what is holding you back. Once you get over those limitations that you set for yourself, you'll find your freedom. The secret to your freedom is not really a secret. If you don't have the audacity to fight for freedom for what you want and when and how you want it, you will have it much harder to move ahead in life. James Arthur Lovell Jr. astronaut (retired) naval aviator, and mechanical engineer once said, "There are people who make things happen, there are people who watch things happen, and there are people who wonder what happened. [19] " So, to be successful, you need to be a person who makes things happen. Don't wait for someone else to make things happen. You control your mind, and don't deny yourself the freedom that comes from simply making things happen. Fight past the "no" and grab the "yes" by the collar and claim it. If you don't do it, don't blame others for your shortcoming.

In life, there are many things that can make it difficult in helping to identify the weakness you have in reaching your goal for your freedom. Some of these weaknesses are your arrogance in life, lack of self-

---

[19] Jim Lovell Quotes. (n.d.). BrainyQuote.com. Retrieved January 27, 2021, from BrainyQuote.com Web site: https://www.brainyquote.com/quotes/jim_lovell_202153

worth and your fears. A lot of times it boils down to insecurity. Your arrogance could be that you are insecure in seeking your freedom by hiding your true feelings by having nothing to learn from others by acting like you know-it-alls. Your lack of self-worth derived from your rejection and disapproval of your goal, because you have no faith in the result. You may realize your fear from the success you might have in achieving your potential freedom. So, If you don't remove these difficulties in helping to identify your weakness, don't blame others for your shortcoming.

To meet a certain criteria or standard in achieving your freedom, you have to understand what freedom mean to you at the unique moment you want to achieve it. While seeking your freedom you must make your feeling all about the right to be different. By focusing on your individual freedom and quality of life you achieve from it, you will experience true freedom when others don't trample on or threaten it. The Declaration of Independence states that we are "endowed by our Creator with certain unalienable rights, including the rights to life, liberty, and the pursuit of happiness." This declaration gave us the freedom in having the ability to choose and be responsible for the way you feel, act, and live your life daily. When you don't blame others for your shortcoming when searching for your freedom, you will have the opportunity to become who you want to be. Achieving freedom is not having to ask for freedom others freely enjoy. This can only be achieved by stop blaming others for your shortcomings. Blaming others only give you a twisted sense of satisfaction that don't always last long. On the other hand, short term, you might genuinely believe that what you're doing is for your betterment, but your issues won't be resolved, and you will be at the same position where you started.

# Is Freedom an Abstract Word?

In our society today, it is said you have the right to speak, act, and think as you want without interference or restraint.  So, can you say that "Freedom is a means to an end, not an end in and of itself. When you have no end and make freedom an ultimate goal, anything goes.[20]" So, how do you define individual freedom in our society, today if it is abstract?  Thomas Jefferson stated that "We hold these truths to be self-evident: that all men are created equal; that they are endowed by their Creator with certain unalienable rights; that among these are life, liberty, and the pursuit of happiness.[21]" Martin Luther King Jr. stated that, "Freedom is never voluntarily given by the oppressor; it must be demanded by the oppressed.[22]" Ronald Reagan stated that, "Freedom is never more than one generation away from extinction. We didn't pass it to our children in the bloodstream. It must be fought for, protected, and handed on for them to do the same.[23]"  Bryant McGill the international bestselling author, and activist stated that "It is better to lose everything you have to keep the balance of justice

---

[20] Biakolo, K. (June 27, 2013). What Is Freedom? thoughtcatalog.com
https://thoughtcatalog.com/kovie-biakolo/2013/06/what-is-freedom/

[21] Thomas Jefferson Quotes. (n.d.). BrainyQuote.com. Retrieved February 6, 2021, from
BrainyQuote.com Web site: https://www.brainyquote.com/quotes/thomas_jefferson_157212

[22] Martin Luther King, Jr. Quotes. (n.d.). BrainyQuote.com. Retrieved February 6, 2021, from
BrainyQuote.com Web site: https://www.brainyquote.com/quotes/martin_luther_king_jr_125901

[23] Ronald Reagan Quotes. (n.d.). BrainyQuote.com. Retrieved February 6, 2021, from
BrainyQuote.com Web site: https://www.brainyquote.com/quotes/ronald_reagan_183965

level, than to live a life of petty privilege devoid of true freedom.[24]"

So, looking at the following statements above by those great leaders and orators can you say that the concept that they used freedom is it an ambiguous or an abstract term?  You be the judge of their contextual usage.  In the United States of America, the country where you live, having freedom means your right to act, speak, and be who you are without the restraint from others.  At the same time, you are free to do what you want without restraint from others, because your freedom is sometimes an ambiguous or confusing term.  You have to understand that freedom exists for you to obtain an objective.  In other word, freedom is the means to do it.  If you can remember your grammar back in school, not to say that you don't use it daily in your speech, you learn that a noun is a part of speech.  A word that identify something is a noun.  Freedom describes something so it is a noun.  As you look at the word freedom mentioned above, it only survives because there is something to be obtain, and it is the means to obtain it.

Upon reading the above quotes, you have to start evaluating what the word freedom means to you.  Thomas Jefferson sees freedom as certain unalienable rights such as life, liberty, and the pursuit of happiness.  Martin Luther King Jr. sees freedom is never voluntarily and it must be demanded.  President Ronald Reagan talks about saving freedom from

---

[24] Bryant H. McGill Quotes. (n.d.). BrainyQuote.com. Retrieved February 6, 2021, from BrainyQuote.com Web site: https://www.brainyquote.com/quotes/bryant_h_mcgill_168244

extinction and, Bryant McGill stated that it is better to lose everything than to live a life devoid of true freedom. Each individual definition of the word freedom as identify with something. These individuals also define the word freedom and invokes their passionate emotions as something of values for you to ascribe to. Freedom is important when it increased productivity and the general quality of your life. When you talk about gaining your financial freedom, it is your sheer determination to have the freedom from living in poverty. Again, freedom is the means to obtain your objective. The lack of or the absence of certain necessity in your life to help yourself, freedom can be that means to an end.

So, in defining your life goals for your freedom you must have set rules that will play a vital role in your search. The rules that you set eliminates all the confusion and misperception that will make your journey orderly. No rules in your search could life lead to chaos and confusion. Don't seek freedom for freedom sake, you must have specific aims while searching, because the rules you set in persuing your goal, will enable you to remove that chaos that come with it. If you don't have any specific aim during your search and if your is only one-way, the result will not be for what you seek but what seeks you. During my research on this subject on-line, I came across this article in the *thewisdompost.com*, "It's nice to think that what you love actually loves you, what you desire desires you, and what you want wants you.[25]" the

---

[25] *Team The WisdomPost & Sophia in Thought. (n.d.). What you seek is seeking you*
*https://www.thewisdompost.com/self-improvement/thought/seek-seeking-rumi/2611*

article further stated that "We are often faced with different situations. Sometimes, we feel like everything is against us, sometimes we feel very happy, and we are not sure if we deserve that. At times, we feel sad, unmotivated, useless, or annoyed. Thinking about our situation makes us think that that is something we deserve, something we were seeking for.[26]" Do you ever have complete freedom to do things on your own free will? If you are acting a specific way that you can't avoid, then your action are not of your own free will. As a rational person, you are granted the ability to act, and think freely. Without this ability you cannot blame others for any restrictions of not thinking freely, you are your own restrictive agents. The restrictive agents are your own fears and doubts that fester in our mind. It is only when you are truly relieved from these agents then you can truly have freedom.

Is the freedom that you desire, your motivating force that drive your actions every day? And what will you do with that freedom once you have it? The motivation you have in acquiring the freedom that you so diligently seek is your driving force. You are encircled by an infinite amount of knowledge and the question you have to ask yourself, is, how and when do I use my personal goals currently as well as in the future? You have to focus on the significance of what you want to achieve, of course you are seeking

---

[26] Team The WisdomPost & Sophia in Thought. (n.d.). What you seek is seeking you https://www.thewisdompost.com/self-improvement/thought/seek-seeking-rumi/2611

freedom, by taking the time to replicate the positive. Marcus Garvey Jr. the Jamaican political activist, publisher, journalist, entrepreneur, and orator stated that, "A people without the knowledge of their past history, origin and culture is like a tree without roots.[27]" Utilize the knowledge that you learn about your past history and freedom is just a step from your knowledge you acquired. Freedom is an abstract word because it only survives when there is something to be obtain, and there are means to obtain it.

---

[27] *Marcus Garvey Quotes. (n.d.). BrainyQuote.com. Retrieved February 7, 2021, from BrainyQuote.com Web site: https://www.brainyquote.com/quotes/marcus_garvey_365148*

# Is Freedom the Knowledge of Necessity?

If you start your battle for freedom from the scratch remember it is because you did not inherit nothing. When you do something on your own free will, it is simply stating that you could have done what you did differently. In other words, you had an option. So, you are morally responsible for the action you take-positive or negative. Mao Zedong, the former Chairman of the Chinese Communist Party stated that, "Knowledge of the world is for the purpose of transforming the world; the history of humankind is created by humankind itself. However, if one has no knowledge of the world then the world cannot be transformed. [28] " So, fighting for your freedom to transform yourself, should be from the knowledge you ascertain from the world in which you live and not from the history created from someone else. Ask yourself the following question before start fighting for your freedom, is the freedom you are fighting for the knowledge of necessity?

On every fourth of July, you celebrate the freedom of this country and this is the day that you celebrate as being free in a free country. Your eventual freedom is often the accomplishment from the endeavor in working for the goal you set for yourself. Your ultimate freedom will always be your independence in your accomplishment in what you

---

[28] Mao Zedong (1987) Freedom is Knowledge of Necessity and the Transformation of the World (1941), Chinese Studies in Philosophy, 19:2, 105-106, DOI: 10.2753/CSP1097-14671902105

desire. Remember, that freedom may be your necessity and may be right for you but not for others. Yes, you may be created equally with others, but your freedom may be unequal. Isabel Allende the Chilean writer stated that, "We don't even know how strong we are until we are forced to bring that hidden strength forward. In times of tragedy, of war, of necessity, people do amazing things. The human capacity for survival and renewal is awesome.[29]"

Searching for freedom does not depend on chance, it is your hard work based on the goals that you set prior. The Knowledge of your necessity is critical in obtaining your freedom. If you work by chance, the road to gaining your freedom will be unpredictable. Walter Cronkite stated that, "There is no such thing as a little freedom. Either you are all free, or you are not free.[30]" Viktor Frankl also stated that, "Even when people in difficult circumstances appear to have no options available, they retain the freedom to choose how they will respond to their suffering.[31]" You must accept the responsibility that comes with freedom, because if you don't, then you are not free at all. So, the freedom you have is not really freedom unless you accept the responsibility that comes with it and it is link to the knowledge of your necessity.

---

[29] Isabel Allende Quotes. (n.d.). BrainyQuote.com. Retrieved February 9, 2021, from BrainyQuote.com Web site: https://www.brainyquote.com/quotes/isabel_allende_599161

[30] Walter Cronkite Quotes. (n.d.). BrainyQuote.com. Retrieved February 10, 2021, from BrainyQuote.com Web site: https://www.brainyquote.com/quotes/walter_cronkite_124506

[31] Excerpt From: Instaread. "Man's Search for Meaning: by Viktor E. Frankl Key Takeaways, Analysis & Review." Apple Books. https://books.apple.com/us/book/mans-search-for-meaning-by-viktor-e-frankl-key-takeaways/id1042804725

Your intention in accomplishing your freedom implies that you have a goal in mind, and you have the knowledge that is necessary in achieving it. You should always focus your intentions on the present moment because it is your driving force in helping you to get there. If your goal in accomplishing your freedom or your specific achievement is not specific, you will be that wondering soul lost in the jungle. David Goggins in his book, Can't Hurt Me, stated the following in achieving his goals, "But facing that mirror, facing myself, motivated me to fight through uncomfortable experiences, and, as a result, I became tougher. And being tough and resilient helped me meet my goals.[32]" In life you have the resilient to endure those stressful moments when they appear in your live. You have to keep an eye on your goal on your journey to get there, and when you overcome those difficult situations, you will have that great feeling of satisfaction.

You have to always remember that your resilience in life is the most important trait in reaching the goal that you set. Freedom is what your seek, your destination, your Goals are your objective to get your freedom and resilience are those attributes you have as your driving force. So, you must adapt those significant qualities that will give you the ability to determine your courage on the way to your destination.

---

[32] Excerpt From: David Goggins. "Can't Hurt Me." Apple Books. https://books.apple.com/us/book/cant-hurt-me/id1446028392"

As you learn to understand that your freedom is the knowledge of necessity when you seek it, because it is your purpose of transforming the world as you transform your life. As your resilience transform your life and change the way you live, you will be more understanding of the actions you take. Mike Bayer, known as Coach Mike, the professional personal development coach and author stated in his book "*Best Self*," stated that, "On any journey, roadblocks are to be expected. They can take various shapes, and they differ slightly for each of us.... If you can see a potential roadblock coming, you can figure out a detour.[33]" So, when you clear that path, make sure you remove all that debris leads to the goal you set, because they may become an obstacle in your way. Don't sweep them under the rug and make sure you don't create any disturbance during the removal. Roadblocks are placed in your way merely to stop you from reaching your goals which is your freedom. In an excerpt from Sun Tzu on the Art of War, he stated that, "If in the neighborhood of your camp there should be any hilly country, ponds surrounded by aquatic grass, hollow basins filled with reeds, or woods with thick undergrowth, they must be carefully routed out and searched; for these are places where men in ambush or insidious spies are likely to be lurking.[34]" In other words, on your journey to your destination-freedom, you must carefully search and remove all

[33] Bayer, Michael. (2019). Best Self. Harper Collins, Ch. 4, p.81, New York, NY: Harper Collins
[34] Excerpt From: Sunzi 6th Cent. B.C. "The Art of War." Apple Books.
https://books.apple.com/us/book/the-art-of-war/id510874085

obstacles in your way.  Remember, you are not placed on this earth to merely exist in your present circumstance because there are always room in your present life to grow.  The Changes that happen in your life while on this earth doesn't happen by accident or pure luck.  It happens because of your hard work.

As you mature in life, you have to remember that the changes you make, you are responsible for them. the goal you set for your freedom will pave your path.  Remember the end goal is the freedom you seek because it is the necessity of your knowledge.  As the Dr. Martin Luther King said,  "Freedom is never voluntarily given by the oppressor; it must be demanded by the oppressed.[35]"  So, the changes that you make in your life starts with demanding the freedom that was never given to you.  Pope John Paul II stated that, "Freedom consists not in doing what we like, but in having the right to do what we ought.[36]"

---

[35] *Martin Luther King, Jr. Quotes. (n.d.). BrainyQuote.com. Retrieved February 14, 2021, from BrainyQuote.com Web site: https://www.brainyquote.com/quotes/martin_luther_king_jr_125901*

[36] *Pope John Paul II Quotes. (n.d.). BrainyQuote.com. Retrieved February 14, 2021, from BrainyQuote.com Web site: https://www.brainyquote.com/quotes/pope_john_paul_ii_178860*

# Freedom is Never Given

You should not take the freedom you have obtained at a price for granted, and you must fight for it every day with your actions and deeds. "To understand political power right and derive it from its original, we must consider, what state all men are naturally in, and that is, a state of perfect freedom to order their actions, and dispose of their possessions and persons, as they think fit, within the bounds of the law of nature, without asking leave, or depending upon the will of any other man. [37] " According to our constitution, you are free and independent by nature and have certain inherent and inalienable rights. These rights are life, liberty, and the pursuit of happiness, and in protecting your rights, a government or institution is there to ensure that others do not suppress your freedom. Even though you are free by nature, you understand that being free is something you always have to fight constantly. The founding fathers' words were written for everyone to observe and obey, but others found ways to usurp them for their interpretation. So, even though your inalienable rights you secure with help from the government, your freedom is never given. And all through the cycle of life, you will be fighting for it. Freedom in life is how you define it.

---

[37] Excerpt From: Eric Mack. "The Essential John Locke." Apple Books. https://books.apple.com/us/book/the-essential-john-locke/id1502143484

Your freedom is not like a light switch where you switch it off and on when you need it. It comes in countless capacities that impact the quality of your life daily. It is more an insight into your desire that allows you to act and speak and accept the responsibility for the outcomes of your actions. In the end, you can deliberate and imagine what you want. Remember, the freedom you seek may come in various packages that are positive and negative. In the end, it is the choice you make. This choice can lead to disappointment because sometimes it may never meet your expectations. In the end, if you fail, all the faults lie in your hand because it was your choice. Remember, the freedom you seek is that notion that you strongly related to the idea of your free will. The late Asa Philip Randolph, an American labor unionist, and civil rights activist, stated that eds. "Freedom is never given; it is won.[38]" He states that you have to fight for the freedom you want in life because you will never get it freely. There will always be a price for freedom, and never take it for granted.

The decision you make for your freedom has to be realistically and individually because of your free will. Your decision changed over some time because it comes in stages. For example, your family's decision is influenced by your family's surrounding at a young age. As you matriculated from your home environment, there are other influences in your decision process. It is the collection of information

---

[38] *A. Philip Randolph Quotes. (n.d.). BrainyQuote.com. Retrieved February 16, 2021, from BrainyQuote.com Web site: https://www.brainyquote.com/quotes/a_philip_randolph_212163*

that you are surrounded by that forces your decision-making process. No matter how much influence you have in your decision, the finality is yours. So, freedom is never given because you choose to follow others' directions or on your own free will. In other words, you have complete freedom over everything you do because your action is shaped internally. Voltaire stated that, "Man is free at the moment he wishes to be. [39]" Remember, you have complete freedom to do anything you want to do with consequences-negative or positive. You are responsible for your own decisions because you are the one who is making them. It is all about your autonomy in life, whether your decision you make is good or bad. When you make your decision freely, you are taking responsibility for your free will.

When you search for your freedom, you must remember that it is your responsibility to steer the right path. Your responsibility in life means you can respond and accept the outcome without interfering with others' will. You have to understand that with your freedom comes the responsibility to respect the freedom of others. Have that vision on how to steer your life by the goals you set. The goals that you select should always reflect what matters most to you. Your freedom does not mean that you can act in any way you please without respecting others. You may disagree with others' ideas, but you respect them for seeking an end to their means. Your good conduct and

---

[39] Voltaire Quotes. (n.d.). BrainyQuote.com. Retrieved February 17, 2021, from BrainyQuote.com Web site: https://www.brainyquote.com/quotes/voltaire_101437

politeness are necessary in respecting others' freedom, which was your desired result for the mean to your end. It is the critical aspect in which the solution to the problem you seek can be described. Therefore, finding the proper sequence of your actions that lead to your desired goal must be your priority. When President Lincoln issued the Emancipation Proclamation in 1863 to liberate the slaves in those rebellious states, he declared them free forever. Even though the slaves were said to be free in 1863, today, their descendants may not be in chains; still, they are enslaved through other circumstances because the influence of slavery continues to have a lasting impact on their generation. These descendants have not made enough racial progress in many areas, and there is a plain view about any progress. There is skepticism about the prospects for racial equality because this country's leaders have failed to give these descendants equal rights with others. The main question is they will ever achieve racial equality.

Loretta Lynch, the former Attorney General of the United States, stated that, "What matters is that there is somewhere for those who are troubled, threatened or afraid to turn to in their darkest hour. What matters is that there are those who are willing and able to use the law as an instrument of inclusion, of protection, and of freedom.[40]" If you look at how the legacy of slavery still affects these people's descendants, you can see that these circumstances allow them not to be free. Our Thirteenth Amendment

---

[40] *Loretta Lynch Quotes. (n.d.). BrainyQuote.com. Retrieved February 18, 2021, from BrainyQuote.com Web site: https://www.brainyquote.com/quotes/loretta_lynch_765116*

of our Constitution in 1865 ended slavery, which should have meant freedom for all African Americans. But even though they were free on paper by the laws, they lived-in desperate poverty, denied the same education, proper medical coverage, wages as White-Americans, and being the last to be hired and the first fired.  These are only a few of the austere circumstances they lived under.  If slaves were only freed on paper and not in person, Then the question you need to ask yourself, is freedom just the state of mind in every person?  And why are there so many laws that are preventing people from denying others their liberty?  Our founding father and our first President of the United States,  George Washington, stated that, "If the freedom of speech is taken away then dumb and silent we may be led, like sheep to the slaughter.[41]"

---

[41] *George Washington Quotes. (n.d.). BrainyQuote.com. Retrieved February 18, 2021, from BrainyQuote.com Web site: https://www.brainyquote.com/quotes/george_bwashington_146824*

# Is Freedom Just a State of Mind?

If you look at Freedom as a state of mind, then freedom can only be delivered by you and you only. If freedom is your state of mind don't look for it on the outside because you are responsible for your action and reaction of others and the way you live your life. It is your rights to place that thought of yours into action without interference and under any circumstances. Dana Damara astrologist and Shamanic healer, wrote the following, "How free you are can be directly related to how free your mind is from being sucked into the drama, circumstance and issues of others.[42]" Your state of mind determine your freedom as long as you do not let others decide and interfere with your thought process. You are the master of your own fate and be in complete control of what happens to you minute by minute. You have to understand that your mind is very powerful, and it is a terrible thing to waste. Yet, you probably spend little or no time reflecting on your thoughts.

Napoleon Hill an American self-help author, stated that, "What the mind of man can conceive and believe, it can achieve.[43]" The way you think about who you are and deflect those negative thoughts and turn positive ones into your reality, you can have a more conclusive idea on who you are and your

---

[42] Dana Damara. (n.d.). Freedom is a State of Mind. gaiam.com. https://www.gaiam.com/blogs/discover/freedom-is-a-state-of-mind

[43] Napoleon Hill Quotes. (n.d.). BrainyQuote.com. Retrieved February 19, 2021, from BrainyQuote.com Web site: https://www.brainyquote.com/quotes/napoleon_hill_258563

capability in engaging the world around you. In the process, there will be no limit to your potential. So, your thoughts are the incentive that you will need to forge your way to the goals that you have decided to get to that end results-your freedom. Remember, your mind is that driving force that directly influence your feeling and your feeling transposed on how you behave in society. If you think that you are not free you will not act like a free person. Hill goes on to say that, "The majority of men meet with failure because of their lack of persistence in creating new plans to take the place of those which fail.[44]" You will become dependent on others and this will emphasize that you are failure in life. Then, the question you will have to ask yourself, if you are a failure in life, is being free just a state of mind?

Failure in life is not the end of your existence. You have to remember, the more you fail at what you do, this helps to build your resilience. You can say that the more you fail the more resilient you will be in making sure that you succeed. In order to achieve great success, you will have to learn that proper planning leads to a better result in what you do. Reinhold Niebuhr the American Reformed theologian and professor stated the following, "God grant me the serenity to accept the things I cannot change, the courage to change the things I can, and the wisdom to know the difference.[45]" So, if you plan right, failure

---

[44] *Napoleon Hill Quotes. (n.d.). BrainyQuote.com. Retrieved February 19, 2021, from BrainyQuote.com Web site: https://www.brainyquote.com/quotes/napoleon_hill_101794*

[45] *Reinhold Niebuhr Quotes. (n.d.). BrainyQuote.com. Retrieved February 19, 2021, from BrainyQuote.com Web site: https://www.brainyquote.com/quotes/reinhold_niebuhr_100884*

will not be your option. If it does, you will have to accept the things that you cannot change, the courage to change the things you can, and the greater wisdom to know the difference. In other word, be resilience in what you do. Please, you must understand that no one owes you anything in this world and if you look all around you, the things you observed are only temporary. So, the freedom that you are seeking if it is only a state of mind, is it just temporary?

Your freedom or liberty is too precious for anyone to infringe upon them or you even giving it up. Benjamin Franklin, One of our Founding Fathers wrote the following, "Those who would give up essential Liberty, to purchase a little temporary Safety, deserve neither Liberty nor Safety.[46]" Even though Franklin's quote is in a different context in searching for your freedom, it fits the criteria of giving up that freedom you valiant fought for. During your journey for that freedom, you have to focus on what you have learned in the process. You have to watch where you are going, because you don't have to walk through a fire to get burn in process. You learn from the reaction of others getting burn. Don't give up that essential liberty for temporary safety. The moral is, if you watch a person go and touch a hot stove and scream from the burn, you will not touch that hot stove. So, the liberty or freedom that you obtain is too precious for you not to fight for it because the cost of losing it will be too much of a burden for you to bare. You have

---

[46] *Benjamin Franklin quotes. (n.d.). https://wisdomquotes.com/liberty-safety-benjamin-franklin/*

to really understand what your life would be without being free or living in a society where your freedom is taken for granted or living in a society where your freedom is controlled by an individual or external force.  Because of the society in which you are living in today, you could only imagine living with virtually no freedom as a citizen.  In the process of doing so, remember those brave men and women who fought, and many gave their life so that you can be free.

Everyday that you open your eyes you must appreciate the degrees to which your liberty has not been curtailed.  Your freedom is the state of your existence of being free to be yourself and enjoy happiness in the process.  Remember, laws in our society are not there to curtailed your freedom, it allows you to be safe. Understand that your liberty or freedom is not a right to do as you please, but an opportunity to do what is right.  It should be your mission to move forward with the goals that you set for that journey to your freedom.  Remember as associate justice of the Supreme Court Louis D. Brandeis said, "Publicity is justly commended as a remedy for social and industrial diseases.  Sunlight is said to be the best of disinfectants; electric light the most efficient policeman.[47]"  Yes, your freedom may be only the state of your mind, but it is important to understand that transparency and openness which are key ingredients to build accountability and trust which are fundamental human right.  So, if freedom is a state

---

[47] Louis D. Brandeis Quotes. (n.d.). BrainyQuote.com. Retrieved February 22, 2021, from BrainyQuote.com Web site: https://www.brainyquote.com/quotes/louis_d_brandeis_402349

of mind, then what does it mean to you? It is your state of mind and the answer can only be defined by you. As Norman Vincent Peale the American minister and author wrote, "Watch your manner of speech if you wish to develop a peaceful state of mind. Start each day by affirming peaceful, contented and happy attitudes and your days will tend to be pleasant and successful.[48]" This is how Freedom can be your state of mind.

[48] Norman Vincent Peale Quotes. (n.d.). BrainyQuote.com. Retrieved February 22, 2021, from BrainyQuote.com Web site: https://www.brainyquote.com/quotes/norman_vincent_peale_402116

# The Fundamental Human Right

The fundamental human rights are those rights that you have, regardless of your race, sex, nationality, ethnicity, language, religion, or any other status. These rights include your life, liberty, freedom of opinion, and expression backed by the constitution. **According to *Article 1 of the Universal Declaration of Human Rights (UHDR) by the United Nation*,** "All human beings are born free and equal in dignity and rights. They are endowed with reason and conscience and should act towards one another in a spirit of brotherhood.[49]" The legal authorities, no matter who they are, may not take away your freedom. You have the right to life, liberty and integrity, personal freedom, and freedom of speech. Your rights are and should be protected by all.

You have the right to life, and it is the responsibility of the law to protect it. Your right to life means it is the authorities or anyone in your community's duty not to terminate your life but to protect it. Protection should be guaranteed except in the situation such as self-defense and others' defense, and lawfully arrest someone. "Self-defense is a legal term which allows a person to use reasonable force to protect him or a third person from personal injury inflicted by another so long as the defender has reason to believe that he or a third person is in serious

---

[49] United Nations. (n.d.). Universal Declaration of Human Rights
https://www.un.org/en/universal-declaration-human-rights/

danger.[50]” Your self-protection is guaranteed under the law as long as the force used for protection is reasonable and justified.

If society limits your freedom, it does not have the integrity to govern you. However, your society is created with individual members, and they have the integrity that allows you to have freedom. Living a life of freedom that is inclusive of integrity is essential to your existence. How can one exist without the other? How can one be true to oneself without having integrity? But in a contradicting role, you can still have freedom without integrity. Yes, you can have integrity without freedom, and you can also have freedom without integrity. But the question that you must ask yourself is, what is a life worth without both? The problem then, what kind of freedom would that be? According to Robert Nesta Marley, the Jamaican reggae singer, songwriter, and musician stated that “The greatness of a man is not in how much wealth he acquires, but in his integrity and his ability to affect those around him positively.[51]” Your integrity gives you the ability to treat others with respect. If others may disagree with your decision, but because of your goodness, respect you for your decision. So, with that said, without integrity, what kind of freedom would you have? Bob Dylan, singer, and songwriter, believes that, “A hero is someone who understands the

---

[50] Erin Chan Adams. (July 23, 2018). what-is-self-defense. https://www.legalmatch.com/law-library/article/what-is-self-defense.htmlUnderstanding

[51] Bob Marley Quotes. (n.d.). BrainyQuote.com. Retrieved February 23, 2021, from BrainyQuote.com Web site: https://www.brainyquote.com/quotes/bob_marley_578991

responsibility that comes with his freedom.[52]" Your integrity allows you to display your quality of honesty and strong moral principles, and your right to act, speak or think without someone placing a restraint on you.

The First Amendment of the Constitution protects your freedom of speech. As stated before, that the First Amendment of the United States Constitution stated that "Congress shall make no law respecting an establishment of religion or prohibiting the free exercise thereof; or abridging the freedom of speech, or of the press; or the right of the people peaceably to assemble, and to petition the Government for a redress of those grievances.[53]" This guarantees that you have the right to express ideas or opinions and information no matter if they are unpopular or not. They are done without any fear of your government censorship. Even though your freedom of speech is treasured, and the First Amendment protects the value and, your government is often at odds in determining the meaning of what exactly constitutes your protected speech. Even though your freedom of speech is considered sacred and constitutionally protected, there are several limited exceptions. Some of these limitations are, you cannot incite an insurrection and threaten others. You have to learn to balance your freedom to speak and understand the harm and present a threat to others. Gloria Jean Watkins, (aka Bell Hooks), an author, professor, and social activist stated

---

[52] *Bob Dylan Quotes. (n.d.). BrainyQuote.com. Retrieved February 23, 2021, from BrainyQuote.com Web site: https://www.brainyquote.com/quotes/bob_dylan_142058*
[53] *1st Amendment of the US Constitution*

that, "The political core of any movement for freedom in the society has to have the political imperative to protect free speech.[54]"

Remember, no legal authorities, no matter who they are, do not have the right to shut down any of your rights or take away any of your freedom. The law should protect your constitutional rights to life, freedom, and freedom of speech. Your right to life means it is the responsibility of all authorities or anyone in your community not to terminate your life but protect it. Your rights are and should be protected by all. The integrity that you display allows others to view the quality of your honesty that can gain the trust. Your relationships with them should base on your transparency, honesty, and mutual respect. Others see you as more reliable and trustworthy. This, in turn, helps you build a constructive reputation by making your creditability in others' eyes. In the process, your integrity opens up new avenues to many opportunities. When you combine your integrity with your freedom, it allows you to display a quality where your honesty and strong moral principles will enable you to act, speak, or think without someone placing a restraint on you. How can you tell someone that the area you saw was a Forrest and when further observation reveal that there are no trees at that location? How will your friend look at your judgement from henceforth? Your words are your bond with others because of your strong moral principles or characters that you display.

---

[54] *bell hooks Quotes. (n.d.). BrainyQuote.com. Retrieved February 23, 2021, from BrainyQuote.com Web site: https://www.brainyquote.com/quotes/bell_hooks_403250*

Liu Xiaobo the Chinese writer, human rights activist, and Nobel Peace Prize laureate stated that, "Free expression is the base of human rights, the root of human nature and the mother of truth. To kill free speech is to insult human rights, to stifle human nature and to suppress truth.[55]" The fundamental human rights that you have are guaranteed. They are the moral principles that describe your conduct's specific standards and are under the constitution's protection. You are protected by laws when you are born in this world. The constitution backs your rights to life, liberty, freedom of opinion, and expression and this document guarantees those rights and sets the rules for your due process of law.

---

[55] Liu Xiaobo Quotes. (n.d.). BrainyQuote.com. Retrieved February 24, 2021, from BrainyQuote.com Web site: https://www.brainyquote.com/quotes/liu_xiaobo_510283

# Standing Up and Fight for Your Freedom

You don't need to be forced to do things against your belief and willpower or do something you don't want. It is not a requirement for you to stand, sit or kneel during the pledge. Your freedom of speech isn't orally displayed; it also can be your actions. Some are buried in cemeteries all around the country and foreign soils, and others are still alive; some are disabled who are even alive with the scars they obtained while defending this country. Our soldiers, marine, airmen were all called on to defend this country and your Constitution and the freedoms it represents, especially your freedom of speech. The task is never easy when fighting for your freedom is never an easy task because it is your right to fight for freedom, and liberty begins and ends with you. Tabatha Coffey, salon owner, and television personality, stated that, "We have to stand up for what we believe in, even when we might not be popular for it. Honesty starts with being ourselves, authentic and true to who we are and what we believe in, and that may not always be popular, but it will always let you follow your dreams and your heart.[56]" Herbert George Wells (H.G. Wells), the famous English writer, laid the foundation on how not to quit when fighting for your freedom. He stated that, "If

---

[56] *Tabatha Coffey Quotes. (n.d.). BrainyQuote.com. Retrieved February 25, 2021, from BrainyQuote.com Web site: https://www.brainyquote.com/quotes/tabatha_coffey_657328*

you fell down yesterday, stand up today.[57]" What are you going to when things are not going your way during your search for your freedom? Remember, you can be a failure today during your search, but you have got to find ways to overcome your failure because it is not an option during your search for freedom.

In order to reach your goal, which is your freedom, you must have the ability to delay those gratifications. Built up your capacity to override all those unwanted thoughts, feelings, or impulsiveness. Use your willpower to exercise your freewill when you face strong opposition or other contradictory signs. You have to make sure that the path that you choose to your goal is feasible by planning ahead and avoid those permanent obstacles. Remember, during your search, look for that road map, which was built by others, because that path you are embarking on, may have been cleared already by someone else. You have to remember that everyone path to freedom is defined on what success means to them and you must only follow a path, if it fits the destination to your goal. You decide to take because no two individuals' journey are created alike. Remember, that ready-made path you decided to follow, may have a different way of fighting the obstacles in in that person's way. So, be extra careful in using other's roadmap and don't get trapped in those dangerous part of destruction of someone else's journey to freedom. Regardless of whether this is your path of someone else, make sure

---

[57] H. G. Wells Quotes. (n.d.). BrainyQuote.com. Retrieved February 25, 2021, from BrainyQuote.com Web site: https://www.brainyquote.com/quotes/h_g_wells_163592

you have the right tools to resist those contagious excitements that surround the journey you are embarking on. So, glance towards your future with lots of confidence, define what the end result means to you and once you get there, fight with all that you got to defend it.

In defending your freedom, how do you fight against those who are deliberately establishing rules and regulations that limits your rights of free speech. The Bill of Rights guarantees that our governments, Federal or State will not establish or make laws that prohibit our free exercise of our speech. You have to wake up and get busy with working on stopping the government from placing you under siege with their laws. If we, don't you will lose your freedom faster than you can ever imagined. So, how do you fight those enemies that are blocking your path? You must exercise that newfound freedom that you acquired and registered to vote. With your vote collaborate with others, this will help you to remove those obstacles in your way. By removing those who want to block your freedom, you replace them with someone who will help to uphold the Constitution and the Bill of Rights. In the process, you let the newly elected person know if they do not uphold the law, you will also replace them with those who will. Beres Hammond, Jamaican reggae singer, made it clear about you giving all today, so you won't regret it tomorrow. He stated, "Give it all you've got today, Follow your heart go out and play, You might never find what you seek, So before you're old and weak, Give it all you've got today. There's a bright sun shining, Shining for you

There's a different morning, Go out and touch the dew.[58]" You might never find what you seek if you don't stand up now and fight for your freedom before you're old and weak and can't fight no more. Please ask yourself this question whenever you past a cemetery. How many individuals went to their grave without achieving their freedom? Fight for it now, not later.

When you wake up in the morning please don't start battling yourself on how you are going to achieve your freedom. By doing so, you you've already lost the battle before starting your day. Instead of battling yourself this early in the morning, start your planning early because this is how you will win the war for your freedom. By starting a battle with yourself this early in the morning, you are about lost even before you even started the day. Fighting for freedom is not the same as battling yourself. We have always believed or was told that we should always battle ourselves and not others. It is not normal to be fighting yourself, unless the freedom you are searching for is within. If you're not free from within and is still searching for your own distinct freedom, you might be looking in the wrong place. If you want to find that freedom you need to search harder by stepping out of your comfort zone. In other words, eliminate those compliant   socially acceptable rules so that you can find your freedom. The question you need to ask yourself is this: Is the place I am at right now, is it good

---

[58] Lindo, A. Hammond, B & Brown, D. (2008). Give It All You Got. Album, A Moment In Time, VP Records, Jamaica WI.

enough for me? Remember, you are striving for acceptance, and you don't have to prove to the world only yourself what does freedom mean to you personally. Freedom has nothing to do with how you look, your race, your creed, appearance, and financial situation. It is standing up and fight for your freedom and not let the government and others infringe on those laws that are guaranteed by the Constitution. Your freedom is your physical and mental well-being in feeling good about yourself in all circumstances and not allowing others to infringe on those rights. Misha Green the American television writer, director and producer stated that, "The story of the Underground Railroad is a thriller. These are people who are basically in a heist movie, and it's the most precious cargo ever, your life. You're fighting for your freedom." Now you can understand that it is your life you are struggling for when you are fighting for your freedom.[59]" So, stand up and fight for your Freedom.

---

[59] *Misha Green Quotes. (n.d.). BrainyQuote.com. Retrieved February 26, 2021, from BrainyQuote.com Web site: https://www.brainyquote.com/quotes/misha_green_1117636*

# Understand Your Struggle For Freedom

You have committed your life to fight for your freedom and build a foundation that you may not have inherited from your past generation. You need to understand this crucial period in your life to fulfill your duty today by understanding how your life is structured, which will help preserve the Freedom you fought and obtain for future generations to come. The future generation must know that their Freedom is through the written words of the Constitution. They need to know that there was opposition to their Freedom even though it was written on paper. Now more than ever, the next generations need to grow up with an understanding of what Freedom means and the cost of winning their liberty. They need to understand the history of your Freedom and how it came about. Expose them to actual events and how they pertain to you. Your story, with all your hopes, doubts, enjoyments, and the key struggles and triumphs you face daily, helped you to fight for your Freedom. Indira Gandhi, an Indian politician, and their first female Prime Minister, in a statement, stated that "All the people who fought for freedom were my heroes. I mean, that was the sort of story I liked reading... freedom struggles and so on.[60]" It is your job to inspire future generations to continue the fight for their Freedom because they need to understand the

---

[60] *Indira Gandhi Quotes. (n.d.). BrainyQuote.com. Retrieved February 26, 2021, from BrainyQuote.com Web site: https://www.brainyquote.com/quotes/indira_gandhi_773268*

history of their Freedom and expose to the actual events and how they pertain to you. During your struggle for Freedom, how do you reveal to the new generation its history? What tool do you use to help define it? What are some of the negative and positive apparent features and their hidden aspects? And who are the players that help you, both famous and obscure? These are some of the central questions you have to keep in mind when engaging others in any historical events. It is also essential how you frame your history in helping them on how to search for Freedom. It is factual that your journey had struggles along the way in trying to secure your Freedom that was not easy. No matter, what happens during your trip, the result should be the start of how to keep your Freedom. Your Freedom is your right to express and access information from all points of view without restricting others. Freedom is the basis for your democratic system, and it is in your Constitution. It is your responsibility as a citizen to be well informed. It will allow you to become a better person. Your Freedom encompasses free will and does not allow the government to establish or make laws that prohibit your free exercise from holding, receiving, and disseminating information.

Your voice as a whole should be an insight into the social, cultural, and political history of your people; no matter what race you are, the struggle for Freedom and equality should be a non-opaque glass for your viewing. You have to instill in the next generation that Freedom has been suppressed from this nation's beginning. Remind them that Caucasians and

Asians came to this country to escape their despotic form of government. The Native who were the inhabitants of this nation were forced from their land and have their Freedom curtailed. Africans were kidnapped from their homeland and brought to this nation as a slave. They have been struggling to gain their Freedom outright. You have to let them know the accurate historical contents when it comes to Freedom. Some people came here to obtain Freedom, others who were here first had their Freedom removed, and many had it taken away. Don't let your conversation goes down the rabbit hole of surreal racism. The facts have to be known. It is about spending time talking about your life's history and how it got to the stage you have to fight for Freedom. You have to let them know that they have to stay informed by knowing what is happening in their government, from the federal, state down to the city councils. Staying informed doesn't mean you stay at home watching the television and read books for information. It means attending your local school and library board meetings. In other words, you must get to know your community and the people who reside there.

It would help if you informed the next generation of the historical contents of the people of other races that live in their neighborhood and other areas around them. Let them know that many Europeans immigrated to this land to escape despotic forms of governments, political and religious persecutions. They came here looking for freedom and a better life. Their experiences were all not the same because they were from different countries where political unrest made them political refugees who wanted to escape from an oppressive government. Their skin color gave them advanced preference over the natives and the kidnapped slaves from Africa. Over the years, the same whites from many diverse backgrounds and cultures who come of their own free will were not treated the same. Some were mistreated. But because of their skin color, they were afforded a set of privilege with advantages and entitlements that gave them benefits and choices solely because they are white. Many of them believe that their skin color made them racially superior, and in their mind, they should control all other races by depriving them of their freedom. They are asserting that they have racial superiority over others through their words and actions.

People of Asian backgrounds came to this land searching for a better life and a new identity in a strange land. Others came seeking Freedom from political, religious persecution, and famine in their homeland. They often find many obstacles while searching for success with their family. In their search for a better life, they had to fight racism and laws that deprive them of their Freedom. Many of these immigrants were taken advantage of by their employers when paid less than other workers. They were many tensions between them and whites who discriminated and stereotyped against them. They were abused verbally and physically because of their looks. The Asians came to this land freely searching for a better life, and in the process, they helped transform the society and culture, but they were often faced with discrimination in fighting for their Freedom.

Indigenous peoples, who are the natives of this land, were the first inhabitants driven from their homeland, hunted and killed by whites. Many indigenous people are still on the reservation, still being discriminated against and harassed throughout their existence on this land. They were forced from their domains, and their treatments by the institutions to protect them continues. There are significant disparities compared to whites in fair treatment, particularly with education, health care, and law enforcement agencies. The widespread centuries of discrimination experienced by the Natives of this land, such as genocides, forced migrations, and segregations, are the main reason why many natives of this land are still seeking their Freedom.

Africans were kidnapped from their homeland and brought to this land as slaves. Upon their arrival, they were separated and put up for auction to the highest bidder. They then became private property where they were bought, sold, tortured, and even killed. They had no authority to make decisions about their own lives. It was taken away from them. They were slaves to their masters who are free to do what they wanted with them. Until this day, they are still trying to regain that Freedom that was terminated. Total Freedom for this group was never a certainty, even though they had few legal protections along the way. Although it was the law of the land, the morally unacceptable of slavery was challenged. After they abolished slavery on paper only, it continues until this day.  Even though they are no longer private property to their slaveholders,  they are still fighting for their Freedom.

Understanding your duty today on how your life is structured will help preserve the Freedom you fought for and won.  This information that you have gathered should be passed on to future generations. The next generation must know that their Freedom is through the written Constitution from their blood, which they should never give away.  They should understand and appreciate the struggle you had to go through in obtaining that Freedom.  Brendan Francis Aidan Behan, the Irish poet,  playwright, and novelist, stated that, "If you greatly desire something, have the guts to stake everything on obtaining it.[61]"

---

[61] Brendan Behan Quotes. (n.d.). BrainyQuote.com. Retrieved February 27, 2021, from BrainyQuote.com Web site: https://www.brainyquote.com/quotes/brendan_behan_134924

# Why Freedom Is Important

Freedom allows you the opportunity to pursue your happiness, speak without limitation, and act in the process without any restrictions. It leads to the expressions of your creativity and inventive thoughts, increased productivity, and it is an overall high quality of life that you pursue. No one should be able to limit those mentioned above. Whenever someone tries to put you into a box, refuse their action and get into your own. Go out there and do your exploration by increasing your value by expanding your circle. Sometimes the most extraordinary occurrences in your life may come in small increments. It is your life and style, and you have the permission to live it the way you want. So, don't ever fear your journey you are on; stay focused and be ready for the next move, and don't let the unknown intimidate you. Remember, it does matter how you treat others along the way and don't burn those bridges. You are not walking alone, and you will always need a route to return and recoup. Your Freedom is essential because, with no Freedom, you are powerless to do many things. Freedom is necessary because without it, you are in bondage, and it is detrimental to your well-being and inconsistent with the laws of nature. Nelson Mandela, South African revolutionary and President, stated that "Our single most important challenge is therefore to help establish a social order in which the freedom of the individual will truly mean the freedom of the individual.[62]" The challenge you have daily is to understand the following. Is the idea of being free a complex one? If so, you must redefine it, and it must defend at all costs.

It would be best if you did not allow others to interfere with the Freedom that you defined. That Freedom is your ideal autonomy to exercise your human power freely. However imperfectly your quest for Freedom is, you must understand that your government has a central role in counteracting private infringement on your rights. The Freedom that you possess is a sacred gift, and no other gift is more significant than your Freedom to live. It is your principles and foresight of how you want to live while being free. There is room for debate over what your plan is and where you want to go, and it shouldn't be controversial. The Freedom you seek must be about educating yourself. An educated individual will help to sustain your environment that is safe and free. This will help to eliminate hostility towards you from others that will create hatred and self-destructive choices. The question you should ask is what it means to be free in a society where everybody cares only about themselves. Your Freedom must not allow others to interfere with your lives, vice versa. It is about reflecting your desire to create a better social condition for yourself. Louis Sebastian Theroux, documentary filmmaker, journalist, broadcaster, and author, stated that "Reflecting the truth sounds easy, but sometimes

---

[62] *Nelson Mandela Quotes. (n.d.). BrainyQuote.com. Retrieved February 28, 2021, from BrainyQuote.com Web site: https://www.brainyquote.com/quotes/nelson_mandela_447261*

it's not.[63]" According to Winston Churchill, "If you will not fight for right when you can easily win without bloodshed; if you will not fight when your victory will be sure and not too costly; you may come to the moment when you will have to fight with all odds against you and only a precarious chance of survival. There may be even a worse fate, you may have to fight when there is no hope of victory, because it is better to perish than to live as slaves.[64]"

In life, if you hesitate in your search for Freedom, you will lose it. So, learn how to move out of your comfort zone at all costs and drop those old habits that made you comfortable. If you are comfortable in what you are doing, you will definitely develop bad habits. When you take on new challenges, you can look back at those previous actions that stifle your efforts in the comfort zone; you should use them as a guide in helping you to get to that turning point of your life. This will help to free and motivate you, and in the process, these acts will help move you to your future. To make it less uncomfortable, move away from being comfortable and seek that Freedom while you are in that zone where you desire that alignment. You have to remember that Freedom protects your right to live, speak, and act following your beliefs publicly and peacefully. It protects your ability to be yourself in our society. Remember, your future belongs to you

---

[63] Louis Theroux Quotes. (n.d.). BrainyQuote.com. Retrieved March 1, 2021, from BrainyQuote.com Web site: https://www.brainyquote.com/quotes/louis_theroux_780601

[64] Winston Churchill quote. (n.d.). azquotes.com. https://www.azquotes.com/quote/523683"

when you start to believe that you can achieve your Freedom. Milton Friedman, economist and Nobel Prize winner stated, "A society that puts equality before freedom will get neither. A society that puts freedom before equality will get a high degree of both.[65]" What is understood doesn't need to be explain; you can't be equal to no one without being free from bondage. The question that you should ask yourself is, how can I be free when I am not equal?

Apparently freedom does not pay in poverty. Your freedom must be related to being happy when your prospect in achieving what is real to you coincide with reality. Can you be free, poor and be happy? Yes, as long as the happiness you pursue is about your liberty and it provide the proper sustainability in your life. The true ultimate feeling in your life is your freedom and happiness is the end result. Remember, you are creating your own happiness by trusting that innermost voice that leads you to the actions you take. This will able you to travel on the road to freedom without letting others dictate your choice of direction. Your well-being and contentment must be your satisfying experience in life. Because being free and happy in life are strongly linked, because freedom allows you the opportunity to pursue your happiness. Your freedom in life should not be a matter of compassion from others. It is your rights and those who govern you has an obligation to make sure that you are able to speak freely to provide for your

---

[65] Milton Friedman quote. (n.d.). Azquotes.com. https://www.azquotes.com/quote/351906?

happiness. The late John Robert Lewis, politician, and civil rights activist who served in the United States House of Representatives stated that "When you see something that is not right, not fair, not just, you have to speak up. You have to say something; you have to do something.[66]" So, being free and happy in your atmosphere should have major influence in promoting a healthy lifestyle. This lifestyle will help combat stress and help to reduce pain from being in bondage.

The power of your lifestyle that your freedom which is define by society allows the right to act, speak, or think without hindrance or restraint from others. If nothing restraints or blocks how you behaves, will there be an absolute chaos in your society where everyone would do as they choose? Absolutely. You can't turn your freedom of choice into an excuse of choice. Imposing your choice of beliefs  on others, makes you their master, because being free don't allow you to diminish your respects for and to others. Yes, being free allows you to think whatever you want, but is it your rights to tell someone you are usurping their rights to speak? You have to understand that letting go of those emotions that are negative towards others are violating your free speech of respecting them. You free to let go of those negative thoughts and stressful emotions but not towards others. It is your free will to act but not in detrimental to others. Viktor Frankl, philosopher, author, and Holocaust survivor in his book *Man's*

---

[66] *John Lewis Quotes. (n.d.). BrainyQuote.com. Retrieved March 4, 2021, from BrainyQuote.com Web site: https://www.brainyquote.com/quotes/john_lewis_810325*

*Search for Meaning*, wrote about changing yourself when challenged. He stated, "When we are no longer able to change a situation…we are challenged to change ourselves.[67]" He further goes on to say that "everything can be taken from a man but one thing: the last of the human freedoms — to choose one's attitude in any given set of circumstances, to choose one's own way." So, no matter what the circumstances are, your freedom can't be taken away because it is important to your existence.

---

[67] *Excerpt From: Viktor E. Frankl & William J. Winslade. "Man's Search for Meaning." Apple Books. https://books.apple.com/us/book/mans-search-for-meaning/id476023633 Viktor Frankl*

# The Circumstances of Your Freedom

Freedom is ingrained in your DNA because the laws of our society govern it. Constantly, you heard everyone talks about your first amendment, your Constitutional right to practice your religion, the right to speak, and even assemble to protest your government to act. All of the above are on display right in front of you daily through the media and written pages. This evolution process not only allows you to transform the physical aspect of your life's journey to the goal you set but equally, your intestinal fortitude or your mental strength that helps your productivity and sustainability. So, when you look back on your learning process's earlier years, you can genuinely say that your people have come a long way, and I am still a work in progress. I am better equipped to forge ahead from the wealth of their knowledge. You have to understand that your journey is not complete yet because you are still trying to emancipate yourself from mental slavery and the status quo that your society placed on you. In trying to be all that you are destined to be, you must live by the fact that this journey is complex and must be conquered. Yes, be thankful and be grateful to those who helped you along the way, but don't forget it could have been worse. Be appreciative of every opportunity and those individuals who have impacted your journey by living in your truth. There are many reasons for the circumstances of your freedom, and no matter what they are, this is your season. Every time you face the unknown, do it with resolve and learn to adjust your mindset in the process. Whenever you meet those fears, turn them into possibilities by changing your mindset. Alice Walker, novelist, poet, and social activist, stated that, "For in the end, freedom is a personal and lonely battle; and one faces down fears of today so that those of tomorrow might be engaged.[68]"

Freedom is essential because the journey to it is your battle. It is crucial because you live in a flux state that is detrimental to your well-being without liberty. Your creator ordained that freedom, and it is not from any man or a Government agency. Your creator is your personal belief, not others. It means that the idea is yours, your own, and for your reason. If your freedom is removed, it is your right to be told why it is. Especially that freedom that those before you have gained, and you have fought for with their life. The freedom ordained by your creator must be an essential part of your life. It allows you to be yourself while working with others to help conserve your autonomy. "A corollary of each person's right to freedom is each other person's obligation not to infringe upon that freedom.[69]" Your freedom is essential because the contrasting version is detrimental to your well-being. In these times of so many changes in your society, you must not forget that freedom means just that—being free. Charles River Editors' book Any Means Necessary: The Life and Legacy of

---

[68] *Alice Walker Quotes. (n.d.). BrainyQuote.com. Retrieved March 5, 2021, from BrainyQuote.com Web site: https://www.brainyquote.com/quotes/alice_walker_146799*

[69] *Excerpt From: Eric Mack. "The Essential John Locke." Apple Books. https://books.apple.com/us/book/the-essential-john-locke/id1502143484*

Malcolm X quoted the following from Malcolm X, "I believe that there will be a clash between those who want freedom, justice and equality for everyone and those who want to continue the systems of exploitation.[70]" In these unique times in which you live, you must look at all things from your perspective, and ask yourself this main question before viewing items from your perspective, What makes exercising your rights more critical than others exercising theirs?

One should always recognize the importance of the circumstances of their power to choose. Specifically, if you have to understand how free you are to select your positions about your own life and in the process, you are subject to all of the circumstances that come with it-positive or negative. Remember, it is all about your freedom of choice. You have to learn that you must not allow anyone to remove your power to choose in all situations that you have encountered. Regardless of the conditions you are in, including experience of injustices, your response in these circumstances matters how you act on them. It is dangerous to compare your circumstances to others because both feelings may not be the same. You are both different individuals. Two people may have the same experiences but would feel differently about the experience they face. Remember, you are not from the same home, and both standards of living are different. Never compare your pain with someone else. You

---

[70] Excerpt From: Charles River Editors. "Any Means Necessary: The Life and Legacy of Malcolm X." Apple Books. https://books.apple.com/us/book/any-means-necessary-the-life-and-legacy-of-malcolm-x/id556294134

may both feel the same pain, but the pain may cause by various reasons. Therefore, both reactions may be different. Your feelings are yours, and you are allowed to have your feelings, whatever they may be. The truth of the matter is you don't know how another person is feeling. You may feel like that person may be living a comfortable life based on your visual interpretation, but that person feeling may be worse than you can imagine. There is no right or wrong way to think about something that happens in your life.

Throughout life, whenever you enter into any situation, certain opinions or expectations will directly influence the way you feel about the experience. None of your experiences will negate the fact that negative things will inevitably happen in some of these situations. Therefore, it is acceptable to have emotions about the situation. It is essential to know that because of your freedom, you are in control, and you will decide how to react to your problems. Your mindsets will always be yours, and you influence at the moment of contact to act or not. You are in control and are the author of your fate. Remember, you are responsible for all your changes, and it depends a great deal on the circumstances. Changes are complex, sometimes can be difficult, and they may come unexpectedly. The consequence of these changes may cause a severe mental and emotional toll on your mindset.

You may have difficulty accepting those changes in your life because of your fears and what they might bring. Your apprehension and the uncertainty that it brings may fuel the loss of self-confidence, one of your basic needs. It may also threaten your peace of mind that forces you to face the unknown, which may be scary. So, accepting changes in your life can sometimes be exceptionally painful and may create an unfilled void. Your hurt may last for a more extended period and sometimes may not erase those negative feelings it made. While going through your feelings, it would be great to have good friends along the way to help you walk through this process. Vocalizing your fears, and bringing them to the forefront of your discussion, will help remove the fuel that has been driving your worries. Remember, your interaction with others may help to reinforce that resistance to change. Motivational speaker and writer Denis Waitley stated the following, "Expect the best, plan for the worst, and prepare to be surprised.[71]" You have to learn that expecting change can be your best preparation, and it will help you be more successful when it occurs.

You must have clear steps that will help to reinforce the change you made. No one can ever tell you that change was going to be easy, but an individual who is on the correct path in understanding the circumstances of their freedom can make their change in their life easier. So, as you reinforce those circumstances, follow the progression those steps to your evolution. In his book Never Enough, Mike Hayes, the former Commanding Officer of a SEAL Team, stated that "When you're in a situation where you are responsible for things more important than

---

[71] Denis Waitley Quotes. (n.d.). BrainyQuote.com. Retrieved March 7, 2021, from BrainyQuote.com Web site: https://www.brainyquote.com/quotes/denis_waitley_165018

your own personal circumstances, you have to remain in control for the good of everyone around you.[72]"

---

[72] Excerpt From: Mike Hayes. "Never Enough." Apple Books.
https://books.apple.com/us/book/never-enough/id1533670181

# Reinforcing Your Resistance

Reinforcing the path on the way to your freedom is basically not allowing negativity to penetrate those barriers you set up during your journey. By putting up those resistant barriers during your journey will help you to realize your dreams. So, in other words your behavior must be reinforced constantly to prevent negative penetration on your path to freedom. During your journey, you need to spend more time with positive people so that their positiveness will have a great impact on you. If you spend more time around pessimistic and negative people, their actions will become yours. In other words, your actions will reflect the company you keep. Regardless of the situation you face, remember your attitude determines your altitude and you can't live a positive life with a negative choice. One thing no one can take away from you is the way you choose to respond to the action others. Your mindset which is your attitude sets the tone for every one of the actions and behaviors that follows you, and this will help to determine the time you take get away from your present circumstance. Blaming, justifying and making excuses aren't going to reverse your situation. By releasing the things that will set you free is letting go of all the blames and excuses. These are the things that will hold you back and keep you away from fulfilling your destiny. Remember your blames and excuses are forge from your hidden desire to manage failure and disappointment that you manufactured. You must remove these actions from blocking your way forward by reinforcing your resistance.

Your failure and fault are inseparable and at some point in your life you have to start admitting that failures mean that you must start taking the blame for them. You will realize in the process that learning from your failure can only be fully realized when you stop making excuses for it. How you respond positively to your failures will ensure that you will try as hard to do your best in the future. You can learn to view your failure positively as a stepping-stone on your pathway to success. The late Zig Ziegler author, and motivational speaker stated that "Failure is a detour, not a dead-end street.[73]" He also stated that it is an event, and not a person. In other word, you must make success your destination and your failure will teach how success leads you back on the right track. The more you fail in life the more elimination you make on your way to success. You must constantly eliminate your failure, and the more you will succeed. So, if you want to reach your goal, you are bound to have failures along the way and in the process learn from them. this is how you will see your success and failure for what they truly are. Even though they are not opposite, they run along the same plain, and help you to achieve success. Are you going to increase your failure rate? Yes, if you want to increase your success? Your failure is what you will actually learn from and with these thoughts in mind, if you don't

[73] Zig Ziglar Quotes. (n.d.). BrainyQuote.com. Retrieved March 8, 2021, from BrainyQuote.com Web site: https://www.brainyquote.com/quotes/zig_ziglar_378594

learn from your failures you will never succeed.  You will be like a hamster on a wheel just churning to reach your success.  In other words, you are always working hard at being busy but never achieving anything that is important in reaching the goal you set.   If you are that hamster working the wheel, then you are an overactive individual working as hard as you can without learning that you are just doing the same thing over and over again, looking for different results.  So, stop doing what you are doing and get off the wheel of failure. Learn why you are not achieving any results from your hard labor.  Stop spinning and start thinking.

Your power of positive thinking is the approach you should take in achieving a more positive and productive outlook in reaching your goal.  Don't think about the mistakes you make (they are just your guides) and think that the best thing is about to happen in your life now.  You are optimistic when positive thinking often starts with you telling yourself positively what you about to accomplish.  If your thoughts that are running through your head are negative, your outlook on your result is more likely pessimistic.  To develop positivity in your life, you must spend more time thinking, talking to others and looking at your surrounding for positives.  By doing this, it help train your mind to think positively.  Over a period of time in doing this, your mind will be obviously searching for positiveness automatically. On a constant basis, let others in your sphere of influence know that you appreciate them by thanking them and appreciate what they do.  This could also be a good morning with a smile and thanking them for their help or advice when it is given.

The point of your power now is in the present not the past. Your life is occupied by ups and downs with certain challenges. You have to understand that your daily anxiety, stress and emotions level that are negative can directly affect your wellbeing. So, stop worrying about the things that you have no control over especially those that happened in the past and others not yet materialized. You have to understand that the best methods in dealing with serious challenges is to place yourself in the present moment. Live in the present, where you have control of what you about to do or say. You have to learn to take on each day and moment one at a time. This is your greatest formula in alleviating or lessen your feelings of stress, and anxiety. You are the person who select the state you want to be in, whether you realize it or not. If you choose to worry about something, you are the one who select it. You have to learn to live in the present moment to eliminate your worries. Worrying is the state that you select when you are trapped in the future or the past trying to control situations you have no power over. The situation is gone and not coming back, and it is not here yet for you to control. Again, put your trust first and learn the strategies of placing yourself in the present moment.

Living your life energetic and resolutely in the present and letting go of the past and not pondering your future. Along with that energy you will be able to focus on what is there right in front of you and stop being the victim of time and truly live in the present moment.  When your mind is dragged into your past or the future, or both, you are victim of the time war and you are now living in the past and not the present. Get rid of your daydreaming of the future and the past. The past and the future doesn't exist and the only point of reference you have is your present existence. College football Mike Leach stated that "If you aren't focused on what's right here in front of you, if you're daydreaming about what might be, you really aren't focused at all.[74]"  Remember that in your present you can hear, see, touch and feel something right now. You can't hear, see, touch or feel anything in the past. It is not here, or it is gone.  The philosopher and religious leader Buddha place it all in context when he wrote, "Do not dwell in the past, do not dream of the future, concentrate the mind on the present moment.[75]" You will have to start accepting your own responsibility by living in the present and use your own capabilities to start here in the now.  Stop complaining about what is gone and what is about to come.  You are in control of your own behavior and you will have to learn to select how and when to react to those situations that occurred.  Start controlling those thoughts and emotions of yours and whenever the past and the future appears, drive them back out and concentrate your mind on the present moment. The point of your power is in the present.

---

[74] Mike Leach Quotes. (n.d.). BrainyQuote.com. Retrieved March 8, 2021, from BrainyQuote.com Web site: https://www.brainyquote.com/quotes/mike_leach_1037813

[75] Buddha Quotes. (n.d.). BrainyQuote.com. Retrieved March 9, 2021, from BrainyQuote.com Web site: https://www.brainyquote.com/quotes/buddha_101052

## When The Choice is Not Yours

It is your choice to conform to society's rules in which you dwell as long as your non-conforming is not against the laws. Then again, it is your choice. As part of confirmation, you don't have to act and live the same way others live their everyday lives. Step away from the conformity that affects your journey and move ahead in your search for freedom. Your intellect may not comprehend the perception early in your journey, but as you move forward and realize that the space you seek is indeed a choice you desire. Positive daily actions are necessary when pursuing a life of freedom. The steps others display are their own, and if you follow their actions, you are mirroring them. If they are struggling, you will follow suit. Do you want to live a life where struggling is the norm? If you wish to sit around like others, you will never succeed in life by doing nothing with your time. Don't preach to the wall about changing your life but never do anything different in the process. Stop, look and listen to your inner self and move away from the state of delusion. Don't be deceived into thinking that someone else is in charge of your life. You are the responsible person, and it's up to you to make change happen. Every morning you open your eyes to a new day; you will have a choice, continue doing the same things that will lead you down the path of mediocrity, or do something that will make you an extraordinary person. If you are not fulfilling your destiny of being what you wanted to be, it is your blunder. Stephen Hawking, a cosmologist, and author stated that,

"However difficult life may seem, there is always something you can do and succeed at.[76]" To move your life to the next level, you will have to stay focused on your dream and find success. So, live a purpose-driven life and have your fundamental beliefs and values to influence your decisions. Remember, your day-to-day activities will determine the significant value of being the person you want to be. Displaying steadfast integrity will warrant the trust and respect of others in your sphere of influence. When The choice is not yours, your life is without a purpose, and you will focus on your weakness and not your strength.

Your success lies within your own hands. Living a successful life is defining what that success means to you. It must be something that you want to help you to determine your fulfillment. In becoming a successful person, you must list all the things you need to do and read them daily. If you want to live a more purposeful life, you must overcome those obstacles by working harder to pursue your goal. Whenever faced with numerous challenges and obstacles in your life, you have to overcome them yourself instead of complaining. You don't want to hear other people complaining about their problems, so why do you want to complain to others? You need to stop complaining and do something about yourself. People don't want to hear your complaining, especially if you are doing nothing about it. You have to understand that thing happens in your life for a reason

------

[76] Stephen Hawking Quotes. (n.d.). BrainyQuote.com. Retrieved March 9, 2021, from BrainyQuote.com Web site: https://www.brainyquote.com/quotes/stephen_hawking_627103

and when it does, you should let it be your teaching moments. You are the only person who can change your circumstances because you are the key to your success. You are the first line to your defense, and if that line is broken, you have no control over that path to your destruction. Always plan your challenge when selecting your battles. Because if you fail to plan, you are planning your failure. Let's face it, you will go through struggles sometimes in your life, and you must have a plan and be prepared to meet them. Proper and prior planning will help with the right decisions in living a successful life. Author Robert Collier stated the "Success is the sum of small efforts - repeated day in and day out.[77]"

You have to understand that success is facing and resolving those obstacles in your way that are there to give you the chance to practice your courage and improve yourself. When you established your goal for that dream you want to achieve or fulfill and keeping that dream alive requires your faith and belief in yourself. You also need that grand vision of yours in the open, place some elbow grease in your hard work, have a steadfast dedication, and that intestinal fortitude that you cannot suppress. All things are possible because this is what you believe and want. You should be excited about life and what you want your life to be. Remember that all things are possible because this is what you believe and desire in the process. Whatever your goals are, there will always

---

[77] *Robert Collier Quotes. (n.d.). BrainyQuote.com. Retrieved March 11, 2021, from BrainyQuote.com Web site: https://www.brainyquote.com/quotes/robert_collier_108959*

be obstacles in your way, and as a positive person, you will look at those obstacles as opportunities to grow or a chance to be creative, while others see them as threats, and they cannot succeed because they are in their path. Once you remove the obstacles out of your way, you will know the difference between your dreams and goals. You have to remember that your dreams are imaginary, and it is the window of your unconscious minds. Based on reality, your plan gives your life direction. You must determine if you want to live in the imaginary or the real world.

In conforming to society, you act in solidarity with the prevailing governing standards and rules to group norms and politics. To achieve your goal, you have to make your dream an actual image. Upon seeing your dream's potential, you will find a way to make it come true by finding the time, a light in the darkness, creating a plan that will have a profound impact in making your dreams come true. You must have patience in allowing this imaginary plan of yours to become a realization. Your vision will never materialize until you take the proper steps toward actualizing them. This is not magic; it is reality, and you must plan and work toward what you want to achieve. If you fail, keep on trying again and again, and don't follow the insanity trail. That trail allows you to do the same thing repeatedly and expect different results in the process. You will face setbacks and many challenges along the way, but don't give up. Remember, challenges allow you to become more creative. In visualizing and planning to make your dream a reality, you need to dream big and continually imagining how to make that dream a reality.  But it will be an imaginary version of your undertaking if you don't act on it.  So, it is good to dream that would allow you to keep visualizing, and this will enable you to focus more precisely on your direction.  Former Seal, David Goggins, asked the following questions, "What are the current factors limiting your growth and success? Is someone standing in your way at work or school?[78]"  You can't let anyone gets in your way in hindering you in accomplishing your goal.  When the choice is not yours, you are allowing someone else to be in control.  Remember, there is only a thin line between your success and failure.

---

[78] Excerpt From: David Goggins. "Can't Hurt Me." Apple Books. https://books.apple.com/us/book/cant-hurt-me/id1446028392

# The Thin Line Between Success & Failure

When you accomplish the commitment you made in the dedicated activity that was your aim in life; you are now flourishing. If you do not achieve the promise you made, you are a failure, and you need to reconnect to those essential dynamics that will lead to your success. Your success in life takes must take on a solid commitment that doesn't waiver or diminish. It is that journey that you are on to claim your victory, and when you come across those obstacles that are in your way, you will have to find ways to remove them from your path. When traveling down your path to success, don't travel recklessly without modifying your course. Remember, recklessness will lead to your failure, and it is not an option to fail when the journey you are on is essential in reaching your destination. With your commitment to succeed in life, you should not have any doubt in your mind, and you will get to your destination without any reservation. You will generate success from the belief that you have in yourself, and you have a free mind with openness to ask for help when you need it. No man can survive on an island alone by themself over a period of time. Seek help along the way and don't let the success you seek become an elusive dream and remember the thin line between you being a success or a failure. Victory will give you that happiness and satisfaction knowing that you have attained the goal you set. Benjamin Disraeli, who twice served as Prime Minister of the United Kingdom, wrote that "As a general rule, the most successful man in life is the man who has the best information.[79]" The success that you attained in life will bring you all the joy and happiness. The late David Brinkley, Journalist and newscaster, placed success in the right context when he stated that, "A successful man is one who can lay a firm foundation with the bricks others have thrown at him.[80]" So, layout a firm foundation with the bricks and not sands that others have discarded.

During your commitment to becoming a successful person in realizing your dream, you must be committed to your task at hand to succeed. Make sure you are embarking upon the task at hand with the expectation of doing it right. It doesn't matter how complex the job is; you will have to find the right way to accomplish it. Even when you fail at the task, you must have the confidence to do it repeatedly, but not the same way, to get it right. It builds confidence, which is good. Remember, failure is a chance to be creative, and it will make us learn, gives us strength and the motivation to do things that sometimes seem impossible. Your inspiration in life will make you understand what your capabilities and limitations are. Sometimes, when you experience success, find ways to review how you get to that level and set your target to pass it. Your failure is there to help you to review and retry again. So, don't look only at your success and condemn it because your failure is also your

[79] Benjamin Disraeli Quotes. (n.d.). BrainyQuote.com. Retrieved March 12, 2021, from BrainyQuote.com Web site: https://www.brainyquote.com/quotes/benjamin_disraeli_134362

[80] David Brinkley Quotes. (n.d.). BrainyQuote.com. Retrieved March 12, 2021, from BrainyQuote.com Web site: https://www.brainyquote.com/quotes/david_brinkley_130590

success, and you will learn from it. All you should worry about is what new experience you had today. The late writer Orison Swett Marden stated that "Success is not measured by what you accomplish, but by the opposition you have encountered, and the courage with which you have maintained the struggle against overwhelming odds.[81]" Your accomplishment, success, or failure comes from the struggle and the hard work on your journey through life.

You cannot make your failure become an integral part of your life. Make it your success. When making your lists of accomplishments and success in life, you should not make failing become that action that threatens your growth. It would be best if you did not put yourself down because you fail at something. Rebound and look at why you forget and use the result as a learning experience and keep on trucking. Remember back in your educational environment, when you fail at a subject or anything, think about how you felt then and the worst thing about it, you had to take that information home to your parents. Now that you have grown and now realize that your failure then was not the end of your life, you survive. That failure was just a letter grade and not a part of your identity. Observe those individuals who never outgrow the notion of their fear and use them as an example. Ask yourself the following question, is their fear of failure impede them from taking risks that would lead them to a successful life? Another question you should also

---

[81] Orison Swett Marden Quotes. (n.d.). BrainyQuote.com. Retrieved March 14, 2021, from BrainyQuote.com Web site: https://www.brainyquote.com/quotes/orison_swett_marden_166019

ask, why are so many people are more successful than others?  That answer should be easy to answer. Successful people fail more at their assigned tasks. You can't succeed your way to the top; you are there already. You failed your way there. Those individuals who are at the top already receive handouts from their parents, relatives, and others. You, in the long run, had to fight failures and others to get there.  Don't ever tell yourself that you are a failure because there is nothing wrong with the path you are taking, and there is nothing wrong with you.  In your journey, you must open your mind to be that successful, and when failure comes along, you will know how to use it for your success. Remember that during your journey, you must leave those obstacles behind but learn from them too.  All those unwelcome failures that tried to make you depart from the right path have now made your journey easier.  Those failures are now success because you have learned from them, and if you come across them during another trip, you will have the tools to defeat them.  So, now you have learned that overcoming those obstacles on your journey will let you know that your failure can lead to a successful journey in life.

Your fear of failure keeps you safe but stops you from trying new things during your journey.  It also doesn't allow you to take on new challenges, and the main thing it doesn't let you take on challenges during new situations. By taking on your fear of failure, it can help you to understand what causes it and the effects it has on you.  On your journey in life, your fear is one of the most powerful forces that will affect your decisions. It also affects the actions you take and the outcome you will achieve. At one point in your life or another, it has been influenced by your fear. On the one hand, fear is your protector, and on the other, it can be an obstacle in your way. Controlling your fear will help you to become successful. Fear comes in many different forms, and the fear of failure is the main controlling factor that will directly impact your success. Professional golfer, Thomas Oliver Kite Jr., known as Tom Kite, stated that "Fear comes in two packages fear of failure, and sometimes, fear of success.[82]" So, overcoming your fear of failure is facing your fear of moving ahead in life; it should be your primary objective while on your journey. Are you afraid of failing at something, so you decided not to try at it? If you don't try to succeed and fail at it, you can now eliminate failure to try from your negative list. Remove that fear of failing that has a paralyzing effect on you, causing you not to do anything. Get rid of your anxiety, and you won't be missing those great opportunities that come along your way. Denis Waitley, the motivational speaker, and writer stated that you must "Change the changeable, accept the unchangeable, and remove yourself from the unacceptable.[83]" He means that you can only change what you can, accept the things you can't change, and stay away from the action of fear.

---

[82] Tom Kite Quotes. (n.d.). BrainyQuote.com. Retrieved March 15, 2021, from BrainyQuote.com Web site: https://www.brainyquote.com/quotes/tom_kite_306366

[83] Denis Waitley Quotes. (n.d.). BrainyQuote.com. Retrieved March 16, 2021, from BrainyQuote.com Web site: https://www.brainyquote.com/quotes/denis_waitley_146906

## Who Has Greater Authority Over You?

No one has no greater authority over your life than you, and all the judgments and decisions you make may or not affect others. Decisions by others also may or not act in contradiction to yours. The laws issued by your government are their opinions. These laws are there to prevent and protect your safety against abuses by others and those who created them. The freedom you have is to make your own decisions and to live with the consequences of such a decision, good or bad. If you blindly obey others, you are a slave to their cause, and your liberty is in their hands. When the government interferes with your freedom by enforcing their will on you, this is call tyranny. When you are on the opposite side of liberty by interfering with the government and others, you have crossed that line; the government will remind you that you are subjugated to them through their enforcement. Gaining your freedom is determined by you, and you don't need to depend on others to direct you along your journey. This is your orchestra, and you are the conductor, and those who want to help with your music must be in tune and play the right note. It doesn't mean you don't seek help whenever you need it; it is only on your own accord. It should be when you desire it. You have got to learn to inoculate yourself against those viruses that are out there just waiting to derail your dream. You not only have to protect yourself from those deadly personal attacks, the dream killer viruses, but also from some of their intricate conspiracy about what freedom is to them.

Remember, it is not about their freedom; it is yours. You will have to learn and understand that you control your destiny, giving your strength. Being in control will remove or help you to avoid those feelings of powerlessness. Visualizing your journey is a must because it will help you understand that you are in total control of your inner thoughts, which can help you avoid being subject to others.

In the long run, taking in advice, teachings, and even guidance from others can help you reach your personal goals. But the ultimate decision to use their help belongs to you. There is no greater authority over your life than you, and all the judgments and decisions you make should not be detrimental to others. If you let others control your path to your goal, the dream is not yours; it belongs to them. How do you achieve your goal without interfering with others reaching theirs? By utilizing your personal development tools. Those are the action plans you set to help you to navigate through the path to success. Even though your actions might be somewhat detrimental to others, you must find ways to navigate around them. You can't surrender your authority over your life because of others and their feelings. Just make sure you find ways to help not to interfere with the common good of others. By constantly setting yourself up by feeling you always need others' input to steer in the direction of your decisions, you will find yourself continuously searching for external answers. You may be at risk of not making the best choices for yourself. As mentioned before, there is nothing wrong with seeking help from others. You must weigh the judgment of your decisions and inspect the path you are traveling closely to make sure the final determination that is made is about serving you. So, in looking for help and guidance while navigating your path to success, you should look no further than yourself. You're your influence because you set your own goal. With the valuable help from others that could be extremely valuable with your journey, you must arrive at your conclusions.

As a part of everyday society, as a human, you sometimes face many difficulties, and you are often taught by your parents and learn from others to buckle down and forge ahead. The more you advance in years, seeking assistance is crucial warranting your progress. In many ways, society carries with it a sense of expectation that should you stumble; you are wholly responsible for making sure you get back up. In reality, few can do this entirely without some support network. In struggling with your problems, you often try to cope with them and conceal them with your coping mechanism. In other times, when you can't cope with the issues you are facing, you will start outsourcing your problems. So, the proper seeking guidance that is agreeable with the direction you are taking can help you move forward. In procuring the proper perspective on your present situation and helping to remove yourself from that negative cycle of distraction, make sure you weigh your selection correctly. You have to become comfortable with yourself during your move to the level by becoming comfortable with yourself and let others know what is blocking your activity to the next level so you can seek help.

If you want to have authority over your life activities, you have to become your self-critic. Being your self-critic can be a good thing, especially during your journey to the goal you set. By becoming your self-critic, you have to contemplate what you are up against and look at your daily performance. Sometimes you can be your own worst enemy, and in many cases, the problems or situations you encountered may be minuscule and are an easy fix. Still, you exacerbate the situation, and no matter how you try to fix the situation, it gets worse. In other words, you are making the small hole into a bigger one. Therefore, obtaining help from others by seeking their viewpoint can be an essential element in reaching the right decision. In other words, they are sharing with you a different perspective from their individual experience. The information expressed can be helpful to you or not. You would have to judge the result given and determine if you want their advice or not. Learning your situation from an outsider's perspective can help you see your trouble from someone else's eyes. The question you need to ask yourself, can an outside view help my situation? That is the question you have to answer on your own. Others may answer your troubles because they went through the exact condition and fix their problems. Remember there is help out there only if it matches your situation, and can you use the opinion of others to make valuable changes in your life? In the long run, if you want to make changes in your life, you can do so positively by following the right direction. In these directions you are taking, you have to identify and understand what you want to change, look at what others have to offer, and in the long run, you have to find ways to eliminate your negativities. The creator of Sherlock Holmes, British writer and physician Sir Arthur Conan Doyle, place it all into perspective, "Once you eliminate the impossible, whatever remains, no matter how improbable, must be the truth.[84]" When you eliminate the impossible, your journey to your know destination will be much easier because you now have greater authority over who you are.

---

[84] Arthur Conan Doyle Quotes. (n.d.). BrainyQuote.com. Retrieved March 19, 2021, from BrainyQuote.com Web site: https://www.brainyquote.com/quotes/arthur_conan_doyle_134512

# Eliminating Your Impossibility

As you journey through life, impossible things happen daily, and you may be wondering why this is happening. You have to understand that whenever things happened that have a low threshold of occurring, that doesn't make it impossible for you to fix. When you make your vision clear and concise and think about the impossibility, remember only doubts entering your mind. Things happen for a reason, and your logic sometimes doesn't prove facts about reality unless you can prove that your reality obeys only your directions. You are diminishing your idea to farce when you claim that you are the only person who can run a mile under five (5) minutes. Only a fool would believe that you're the only miler with that time in our universe. It is just your logic. You have to understand that the basic assumption is that every occurrence is either essential or impossible in this world. If you eliminate the impossibilities, if possible, then you would reside in a world that is all truths. You would need no laws because this would be a peaceful world. You can never eliminate the impossible in the long run, and what you think was impossible could be unbelievable. Once you have established that you can't achieve your dream, you have just eliminated your journey to the goal. Don't forget your dream slayers; they are always around like pests. All you need to do is to bring out the bug spray and eliminate them as soon as they raise their head out of their hole. Their main concern is to disrupt your course of action. Don't let them dictate nor change your course of action. Take command of your space by eliminating those impossibilities. The more you eliminate your impossible, the clearer your path will be to the possibilities. Once you accomplished your mission, there are still lots of options that remain. Clear your approach to that goal you set; your task is to remove those who block your dream and become that possibilities warrior. So, when you have eliminated your impossible, remember what remains, however improbable, is the truth.

Clearing your approach is to remove all that is in your way; this will help from stumbling over debris, the truth slayers while heading in your planned direction. This action requires you to execute a particular approach to your destination. Your specific approach clearance is the goals that you set while pursuing your dream. This information is ingrained in your thought process, and it is your mapped approach plan. Whenever there are deviations from your norms, you have likely known and plan for those adjustments. Remember that you are the controller of your faith in the present moment, and you must not overcompensate your course of action. Whenever you have more than one plan, make sure you are using the more conducive to your journey. You must always adhere to all the guidance in the contract you made with yourself and live by the required terms. Each moment you have built on your practices while on your current path, don't use the established styles that constrain your progress and development. Despite your extensive efforts in promoting and supporting the guidelines you created, barriers sometimes pop up to block your moves. When those barriers cross your path, you must plan to assess the situation by focusing on what works for you—focusing on eliminating your impossibility when those barriers appear.

Despite all your significant efforts to support your journey, you must first clear the negative barriers that are in your way. Remember, these barriers vary across the journey you set and within guidelines that you establish. One of the main things the perceived barriers don't have a specific moment to jump at you. No matter how prepared and coordinate you are for the campaign, no leverage will help you effectively prepare for your journey. You can try to learn from the perspective of others who went on the same journey as yours; doing your dry run to find those areas where you meet obstacles; remember that you are the only one who can best dictate your trip to deliver your plan. While on your journey, don't feel any pressure to use every single or specific technique. Remember, it is the quality of your trip, not the quantity. Everything that you do to prepare you for your journey should fit in your plan. If you fail to plan your journey, you are planning to fail. When it comes to Choosing your goal in life, don't fall for all the stunts that you see. Evaluate all carefully to find one that's right for you. So, before you start identifying your path for your journey, make sure you have a compact plan for your goal. Then you can begin to determine which plan to use, and your back-up plan should the original meet upon obstacles. How do you decide which plan to use? Your quality plan should eliminate your impossibilities.

There is no shortage of advice during the selection of your goal. You can find the information in magazines, books and other people who promise that their plan is the best for you. Remember, the best plan is your plan, and you are the one who selected it. There are so many conflicting approaches out there from others, then the question is, how do you know which system is the best that might work for you? Here are some suggestions that may work for you in choosing your goal. Yes, you can review plans that are similar to yours that worked for others. Remember, what works for others may not work for you. The obstacles they may have faced might be different in your journey, but you may likely find a plan to tailor to your needs. You can consider your personal needs why you are selecting your goal. Make sure you have a safe and effective strategy in helping to accomplish the goal that you set. Remember, there is no specific pre-plan unless you follow the plans of others. Modifying your behavior before entering your journey for that goal is vital and could significantly impact your long-term result. Drew Pinsky (aka Dr. Drew), American media personality and nationally syndicated radio talk show Loveline stated that "What motivates most people to change their behavior is consequences. No consequences? No behavior modification.[85]" Your plan has to be strategic and flexible. This strategy will help you to identify significant problems and make changes promptly when it is necessary to halt or reverse existing issues. You'll likely always have to

---

[85] *Drew Pinsky Quotes. (n.d.). BrainyQuote.com. Retrieved March 22, 2021, from BrainyQuote.com Web site: https://www.brainyquote.com/quotes/drew_pinsky_1095783*

remain vigilant on your journey. So, before you plunge into a journey without direction, always make your plan. Just because your friends were successful with their project doesn't mean it's the right one for you. A qualified plan that you created should help you to eliminate your impossibilities.

# Freedom and Religion

The First Amendment of our Constitution made it clear that "Congress shall make no law respecting an establishment of religion or prohibiting the free exercise thereof, or abridging the freedom of speech, or of the press, or the right of the people peaceably to assemble, and to petition the Government for a redress of grievances." You can see that the first sixteen (16) words of our Constitution made it clear about religion, and the rest of the amendment inform you what to do whenever anyone tries to violate that law. It is your right to freedom in supporting or not to support, change or believe in a specific religion privately on publicly and no one can deny you those rights. Firstly, you must understand what you are free to exercise or from religion does mean. You have the freedom from the rules and doctrines that your neighbors or community members from other religious opinions have. You are free to obey the demands of your conscience or your freedom to follow any religion you want or not. Your religious freedom prevents others who have majority power from using the government to enforce their religious beliefs on you. John Adams, the second President of the United States stated that "Our Constitution was made only for a moral and religious people. It is wholly inadequate to the government of any other.[86]" This also protects you even if you are a religious or

---

[86] *John Adams Quotes. (n.d.). BrainyQuote.com. Retrieved March 26, 2021, from BrainyQuote.com Web site: https://www.brainyquote.com/quotes/john_adams_391045*

and nonreligious person. In other words, the law prevents the government from becoming authoritative that it can side with the majority tell you what to think and how to act religiously. Throughout our history, you have to remember that your First Amendment was always protecting your freedom of religion. Your First Amendment may enforce the separation of your church and state, but it doesn't prohibit freedom and your faith from public life.

History has revealed that religion has played a significant role in politics in this country. When it comes to complicated cases of religious freedom, the Supreme Court has ruled conflictingly. During Colonial times, there were many killings done in religions, mainly by certain Europeans who came from some distinct regions who believe that their religion is the main and their worship is the right one. They would attack and kill other members of other religions, all in the name of the same God they served but from a different perspective. Even though many left their country to escape the suffering from religious persecution, they would not tolerate any other opposing religious views. They believed that their religion is the only sanction one by their God. Religion also plays a prominent role in African Americans searching for their freedom. In the book "His Truth Is Marching On" by Jon Meacham, historian, and presidential biographer and the late John Lewis, politician and civil rights activist who served in the US House of Representatives for Georgia. It stated that "Religious metaphors and religious language form a kind of common bond in America—you can think of it either in literal or literary terms. Even if you are basically secular, the ideals and principles that come out of religion are essentially what we all should share: what is the right thing to do, what is just, what is fair.[87]" Whether you are religious or not, you must believe that it is the right thing to do in your search for freedom because there is no other alternative. You must share what is just and what is fair on your journey because the moral values you possess originate from sacred texts of each of the respective religions. For example, Caring for one another is a religious moral based on your values and principles of love, which you don't need a bible to teach you. Robert Casey Jr., An attorney and United States Senator from Pennsylvania, placed it all in context when he stated, "Your moral values replicate your beliefs and practices which has a religious connotation to them, and these are the same ideals and principles that are essentially what you share.[88]" Your Freedom and Religion made your creation, and the principles you learn from it are unique to all religious and non-religious people. These principles allow you to share a special relationship with others in your community.

Whether or not you hold any religious or non-religious belief, the freedom you have will help to bring you hope and consolation. If you have any difficulties defining who you are, your freedom will be diminished in your continuing struggle to protect it. So, You have the right to your liberty and religion, and

---

[87] *Excerpt From: Jon Meacham & John Lewis. "His Truth Is Marching On." Apple Books. https://books.apple.com/us/book/his-truth-is-marching-on/id1513817814*

[88] *Robert Casey Quotes. (n.d.). BrainyQuote.com. Retrieved March 26, 2021, from BrainyQuote.com Web site: https://www.brainyquote.com/quotes/robert_casey_288868*

it is your freedom to decide what religion you want and change your religious belief. No government can force you to adhere to a specific religion or stop you from joining and changing religion. Thomas Paine, a political activist in his book, Common Sense, stated that, "Securing freedom and property to all men, and above all things, the free exercise of religion, according to the dictates of conscience; with such other matter as is necessary for a charter to contain.[89]" What is true and what is righteous for you may not be for your Government. So, when your Government in the process wants to reject your freedom or the country's political plurality, leaving the rules of laws, and where the power to rule is in the hand of one person, this is an Autocratic form of Government. That Government can reject your freedom to exercise your religion. In a democratic form of Government, when there is an interest at stake for the Government, they can limit your religion's free exercise through the Supreme Court. The supreme court sometimes favors the Government and has upheld and limits to free exercise of such. So, in both autocratic and democratic forms of Government, the leader can limit your freedom to exercise your religious view. In your democratic form of Government, the free exercise clause in the first amendment prohibits your Government, in most instances, from interfering with your practice of the religion you prefer and protects your religious beliefs. The founders of this country were from different European countries who were of

---

[89] Excerpt From: Thomas Paine. "Common Sense." Apple Books. https://books.apple.com/us/book/common-sense/id395535318

different religious backgrounds themselves. They believe that the best way to protect your religious liberty is keeping the Government out of religion. The First Amendment was created to guarantee the separation of church and state and allow you the freedom to be a religious or non-religious person.

# Conclusion

With your thorough examination before embarking on your journey to search for your freedom, you will need to understand better where and what direction you want to go. A better understanding from a previous search will help to start living your life the way you want without the fear of interruption from others. You will now understand that being free in life enables you to pursue your passion and do the things you love. The key to your understanding is that freedom means different things to each individual, and your result should be your highest priority. Differentiates the meaning of freedom is from and individual perspective. Therefore, because the meanings are different for each individual, you can't sit back and wait for the end result from others. You will have to fight for your freedom because the struggle for it always begin internally.

There are times when you see, feel and hear the truth about yourself from someone else and you become enraged with anger, filled with stress that lead you to be disconnected from yourself. You can't let anyone freedom becomes your priority in life. Remember, this world is full of ideas and you need your own protective layer. Sometimes you may disagree with someone else, does not mean that your disregard their idea of freedom. You need to understand that in your society when searching for your freedom, your temperament in you search leads the way to a stronger performance and it is your determination, and that willpower is that indication to become successful.

Your journey to freedom can be a hazardous one that sometimes will get you tired mentally, physically, and emotionally drained. But to complete your journey, you have to put the pedal to the metal and keep it ongoing. You got to understand that nothing good comes easy and without a cost. As Theodore Roosevelt, the 26th President of the United States, said, "Nothing in this world is worth having or worth doing unless it means effort, pain, difficulty. No kind of life is worth leading if it is always an easy life. [90] " Stop working in the easy lane of life. Remember, it will be crowded with others in this lane, just like you seeking the easy way in life. If you get a breakdown during your time of traversing, no one will stop to help you. They will ask, why is he breaking down on this easy road? No one will attempt to bully you into silence in the problematic lane of life because they are too busy with their travel. You would never allow anyone to intimidated you into silence, nor would you allow yourself to be made a victim of circumstance. You will be brave enough and will not accept or let anyone define your goal-your freedom. So, go ahead and describe yourself as you are on your journey. You have to learn to dislodge all your fears as only you understand them, live in your moment, and learn as you travel to let your journey subside your worries. Nigel Mansell, a former champion racing car driver, said, "I think life is full of challenges and

---

[90] Theodore Roosevelt Quotes. (n.d.). GoodReads.com.
https://www.goodreads.com/quotes/8242539

problems. I don't believe that anyone is perfect. We all make mistakes. It's not a bed of roses, and you have to work really hard at it.[91]"

In the pursuit of your freedom, You must have that passion for doing what you love, and it must be your highest priority. Find ways to change your attitudes about yourself by learning to understand your inner perception. Remember, your struggle is always internally, manifest itself visually, then find ways to the outside. You will have to find ways to determine what happens when you are struggling with cohabiting conflicts internally, which creates a feeling of being trapped, and you have no way of winning in that situation. You will have to learn how to be mindful of how you feel and find a proper working solution that will help you work your way through the problem. By being kind and gentle in understanding your situation, will help you to resolve your issue. Determining your solution will allow you greater leverage in seeking your freedom guaranteed by the First Amendment of the United States Constitution. Remember, this is the same freedom that is guaranteed to all who seek it, and if you want to be successful at it, you should never let it overcomes you. If you're going to be a success, you have to believe that successful people never let fears overcome them on their way to freedom; it was their motivation. Sitting at home crying for freedom without taking action will not give you any satisfaction that will guarantee a path to your goal.

---

[91] Nigel Mansell Quotes. (n.d.). BrainyQuote.com. Retrieved March 28, 2021, from BrainyQuote.com Web site: https://www.brainyquote.com/quotes/nigel_mansell_308447

The moral compass that embodied your values and belief system are the principles that allow you to set and define your goal. These systems, when ingrained, won't let you blame others for any shortcomings. It helps to identify who you are and ways to reach your goal by strengthening that resolution. It also encourages you to dig deep into your intellect and search for what you want, including your fear and the barriers that are holding you back. This will help you to realize you can eliminate the fear you have holding you back from your success. It helps to clear your path of all the negativities and help you to achieve your potential freedom. The only power that you have is in your present moment. It is not in your past because it is irrelevant, and it is not in your future because it is unpredictable. Having your freedom doesn't give you the right to act and speak whatever you want. It only means that the Government can't infringe on your rights or take action that interferes with your requests. This can be an ambiguous or confusing term. The Government can infringe on certain rights because they have the power of an eminent domain, which allows them to take your land for public purposes only and provides fair compensation. You also can't use your freedom to denied others of their rights to be free. You can express your feelings as long as they do not interrupt others' activities or the organization. The freedom you achieve will always be your independence in the accomplishment of what you desire.

To eliminate the impossibility in your life while searching for your freedom, you must have a clear and concise vision. Remove all those interruptions in your life so that you can focus on the remains. These remains are highly possible and are the solutions to your problems. Remember, it is your right to make your own decisions and to live with all the consequences of such a decision, good or bad. If you blindly obey others, you are a slave to their cause, and your liberty is in their hands. So, you have to remember that freedom is not externally; it is how you feel inside about yourself. Forest Whitaker, Actor, producer, and director wrote the following about internal forces. He stated that, "Many of the wars we see around the world start as domestic conflicts that are fueled by external forces and powers. My view is that we can help peace if we help communities transform from the inside, on their own terms.[92]" Therefore, crying for freedom is not being free because there are always external forces that will constantly interfere with you. Go ahead and search until you find the highest value of your life, which is your freedom without any external implications.

<hr>

[92] *Forest Whitaker Quotes. (n.d.). BrainyQuote.com. Retrieved March 28, 2021, from BrainyQuote.com Web site: https://www.brainyquote.com/quotes/forest_whitaker_824941*